Control
Alcoholism

With Amino Acids & Nutrients

Billie J. Sahley, Ph.D., C.N.C.

Katherine M. Birkner, C.R.N.A., Ph.D.

Jule Freeman, C.N.C.

Pain & Stress Publications®
San Antonio, Texas
March 2005

Copyright © 2005 Pain & Stress Publications®

Notes to Readers

This material is not intended to replace the services of a physician, nor it is meant to encourage diagnosis and treatment of illness, disease, or other medical problems by the layman. This book should not be regarded as a substitute for professional medical treatment and while every care is taken to ensure the accuracy of the content, the authors and the publisher cannot accept legal responsibility for any problems arising out of experiementation with the methods described. Any application of the recommendations set forth in the folowing pages is at the reader's discretion and sole risk. If you are under a physician's care for any condition, he or she can advise you whether the programs described in this book are suitable for you.

No part of this publication may be reproduced, stored in a retrieval system, or transmitted in any form by any means, electronic, mechanical, photocopied, recorded, or otherwise, without the prior written permission of the authors.

This publication has been compiled through research resources at the Pain & Stress Center, San Antonio, Texas 78229.

1st Edition
Printed in U.S.A.

Additional copies may be ordered from:
Pain & Stress Center
5282 Medical Drive Suite 160 San Antonio, Texas 78229-5379
1-800-669-2256 or visit http://www.painstresscenter.com

Library of Congress Control Number 2005901400

ISBN 978-1-889391-30-1

Dedicated . . .

To a new generation of physicians, therapists, and educators who seek to find the natural alternative that frees the addicted from the prison of prescription, alcohol, and street drugs, and gives them God's greatest gifts—the freedom to make a choice.

To my beloved mother, who started me on the path to understanding the power of the mind and using it.

To a little boy named Scooter, now an angel in heaven.

And to the Lord for always lighting our paths.

Acknowledgements

Our sincere appreciation and thanks to:

The staff of the Pain & Stress Center of San Antonio for their support and dedication to helping people with addiction problems.

Linda Volpenhein, C.N.C. and Laura V. Boone, C.N.C. (candidate) for their countless hours of research and assistance to help make this book a reality.

The many physicians and therapists across the country using orthomolecular medicine who share their research and give us constant encouragement.

Our patients who teach us something every day.

Table of Contents

Introduction	9
1. Alcoholism	11
Progression of Drinking Symptoms	12
Are You Hooked?	13
Acute Alcohol Withdrawal	14
Alcohol Withdrawal Syndrome	15
Symptoms of Alcohol Withdrawal (Mild or Early)	16
Symptoms of Alcohol Withdrawal (Late)	17
2. Genetics	19
3. Neurotransmitters	23
The Synapse	23
4. Alcohol's Effect on Neurotransmitters	26
5. Alcohol Metabolism and Acetaldehyde	29
6. Nutrition and Alcoholism	33
Factors Leading to Malnutrition in Alcoholism	34
Alcohol/Drug Induced Nutritional Deficiencies	35
7. Hypoglycemia, The Sugar Connection	38
Symptoms of Low Blood Sugar	38
Sugar By It's Many Names	39
8. Candida	41
9. Amino Acids and Nutrients, The Keys to Recovery	42
10. What Amino Acids Do and Why We Need Them	44
Dopamine and Tyrosine	46
GABA	47
Endorphins and DLPA	48
Glutamine	48
Branched Chain Amino Acids	49
Super Balanced Neurotransmitter (SBNC)	50
T-L Vite	50
Vitamin C	50
B Complex	51
Essential Fatty Acids	52
Fatty Acids	52
Magnesium	54
Symptoms of Magnesium Deficiency	55
Calcium	56

Zinc	57
Super Pancreatin	57
Decaf Green Tea Extract	57
L-Theanine	58
Alpha Lipoic Acid	58
Taurine	59
11. Withdrawal Support, It's About Nutrition	60
Optional Supplements	61
Nutrient and Amino Acid Program for Withdrawal 3 Months Post Sobriety	62
Alcohol Maintenance Program Nutrients	64
12. Beyond Supplements	65
Sugar	66
Caffeine	67
Nicotine	67
The Cortisol Connection	68
13. Getting Started	69
Beyond Supplements, Strategies for Maintaining Sobriety	70
Alcoholics Anonymous	70
Friends	70
Exercise	71
Body and Brain Profile Tests	72
Food Allergy Profile	73
Essential Fatty Acid Profile	73
Comprehensive Vitamin Profile	73
DHEA Sulfate Level	73
Bibliography	74
Index	76
Consultation Service	78
Other Books by Pain & Stress Publications®	79
About the Authors	80

Introduction

Jennifer, a 32-year-old teacher, after a nutritional consultation, purchased some products from the Pain & Stress Clinic. She called to report the products she tried were very helpful in relieving her anxiety and depression. She noticed that along with an improvement in her mental state, she was drinking much less and simply, did not desire to drink. Her life-long pattern was to drink to excess when she was under stress. She wanted to know if this decreased desire for alcohol was her imagination, or if the supplements could have this effect.

Certain amino acids do stop alcohol craving. Briefly, I explained the brain chemistry involved in alcohol craving. Amino acids function as neurotransmitters (the chemical messengers in the brain) and that low levels of certain neurotransmitters create the brain chemistry of craving. Stress, especially prolonged periods of stress, uses up available stores of neurotransmitters leaving us depressed, anxious, and craving alcohol or other substances for relief.

She said most of her family was just like her, drinking too much, with classic symptoms of depression and anxiety. I told her that didn't surprise me as alcoholism is a metabolic disease, often genetic in origin. Commonly, you see several generations of a family having similar problems. The same biochemistry that leads to alcoholism can also manifest as Attention Deficit Disorder, depression, or anxiety disorders. Jennifer was amazed by the information and her own recent experience with decreased craving confirmed what I was telling her was true. We talked about the connection between depression and alcoholism and how her brain chemistry contributes to both problems. You could hear the excitement in her voice as her understanding began to fall into place. She was excited to learn that these simple supplements were the answer to a 10-year problem with alcohol.

Our hope in offering this book is that you too will begin to understand the connection between neurotransmitters, alcoholism, genetics, and nutrition. You will see alcoholism and alcohol abuse as the metabolic disease it is, and viewed, as a metabolic disorder, alcoholism becomes very treatable. If you eat an appropriate diet, take the correct supplements to balance brain chemistry along with a twelve-step program, such as Alcoholics Anonymous, you can truly control your life.

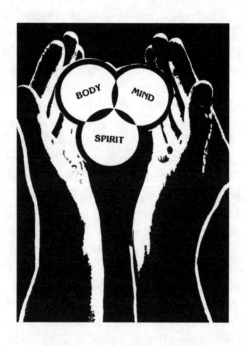

1
Alcoholism

When you think of alcohol many different thoughts come to mind. For some, alcohol is an enjoyable addition to a social setting—a glass of wine with dinner and friends, or a beer while watching the game with the guys. When used in that context, moderately and socially, alcohol actually has many positive health benefits ranging from better adult psychological health—due to alcohol's anti-anxiety properties—and increased life expectancy. Research has shown moderate drinkers (one or two drinks daily) live longer than both abstainers and heavy drinkers.

Some of alcohol's proven health benefits for moderate drinkers are lowered LDL cholesterol (the bad cholesterol) with higher HDL (healthy cholesterol) levels, prevention of the formation of blood clots, and increased estrogen levels in postmenopausal women. The positive health benefits for moderate drinkers are so great that Dr. Robert H. Fletcher of Harvard Medical School stated in the *British Medical Journal*, "On the basis of this (referring to alcohol's health benefits) and other information…clinicians probably should behave as if moderate alcohol intake is, on average, not just harmless but beneficial."

With all these health benefits you wonder if we all shouldn't take a drink daily along with our multiple vitamin. The answer to that is a loud, emphatic no! Moderate alcohol consumption is one drink a day for women, and two for men. Going over that healthy limit quickly changes alcohol's health benefits to serious health risks and for a great many of us the temptation to exceed the limit is too overpowering.

The other, and all too prevalent, end of the idyllic picture of romantic dinners sipping wine is alcohol dependence or alcoholism. In the middle ground between healthy alcohol consumption and alcoholism lies the murky water of alcohol abuse—the person who is not dependent, but who drinks too often, or too much when they do drink. Alcohol abuse, like alcoholism, carries serious health and social risks.

Alcoholism is one of the most pervasive diseases in the United States. Alcoholism does not discriminate, cutting across gender, race, age and nationality. Approximately 15.4 million adults have serious alcohol-related problems. Teens and adolescents rate a close second with 4.6 million having serious alcohol-related problems. Alcohol is an addictive substance (drug). Alcoholism is ranked the number two killer in this country behind cancer and many believe alcoholism actually outranks cancer. Alcohol affects 65 million in the U.S. As with most drug abuse, it affects not only the alcoholic, but has disastrous consequences for family, employers, and society in general. Alcohol is the number one drug of abuse in the U.S., costing the economy in excess of $200 billion every year.

According to the National Council on Alcoholism and Drug Dependence about 14 million Americans abuse alcohol. Alcohol is also the number one drug of choice among American youth. One in every three adolescents have experienced bad effects from

Progression Of Drinking Symptoms

Development Stage	Overt Alcoholism	Deterioration Stage
Social drinking	Loss of control	Vague fears
Once a week	Before breakfast	Prefers solitary life
Drinking faster than associates	Protects supply	Delirium tremors
	Weekends lost	Insomnia
Blackouts (memory)	Solitary drinking	Loss or depletion of vitamin stores
More drunk than associates	Will not share thinking or ideas	
Avoidance of family closeness	Decreased tolerance	Death

Are YOU Hooked?

Adapted from the National Council on Alcoholism's self test, the following questions are designed to point out problems with alcohol.

Do you sometimes binge on alcohol or drugs?

When drinking, does your personality change?

Are more people treating you unfairly without good reason?

While you are drinking, do you avoid family or friends?

Do you become irritated when friends or family discuss your drinking?

Do you feel guilty about your drinking?

Do you feel sorry about things you said while drinking?

Has excess drinking ruined special occasions?

Do you frequently fail to keep promises you have made to yourself about reducing or controlling your drinking?

When you are drinking, do you eat very little or sporadically?

Do you feel depressed after indulging, and sometimes miss appointments or work?

Do you drink more and more to get drunk?

"Yes" answers suggest that you need help. Contact an orthomolecular or nutritional medicine specialist.

alcohol use, ranging from poor school performance to legal trouble. Alcoholism is a progressive disease and is estimated to reduce an individual's life expectancy by 10 to 12 years, if left untreated. Each year more than 100,000 Americans die of alcohol-related causes. Sadly, alcoholism is one of the most common preventable causes of death among Americans.

Acute Alcohol Withdrawal

Withdrawal symptoms start four to twelve hours after reducing or stopping alcohol. Research demonstrates the peak period for withdrawal is one to three days with the duration of five days to seven days. Symptoms of withdrawal from alcohol are excitatory and can include symptoms of hyper arousal from the sympathetic nervous system.

Symptoms of Alcohol Withdrawal

Physical signs: body and hand tremors, elevated blood pressure, tachycardia, dilated pupils, increased body temperature, seizures, restlessness, hyperactivity, agitation, ataxia.

Mental symptoms: anxiety, panic attacks, depression, paranoid delusions, illusions, disorientation, and visual hallucinations, inability to focus, OCD behavior.

For Acute Withdrawal Use

GABA 750 mg – Dissolve in 8 ounces of water, 3 times daily.

Mag Chlor 85 – 15 to 25 drops, twice to three times daily along with

L–T (Theanine) – open 2 capsules and dissolve in water, then add some fruit juice and Mag Chlor, 2 to 3 three times daily.

Mood Sync – 2 capsules, 3 times daily. *(NOTE: Do not use if you are taking tricyclic, MAO, or SSRI antidepressants. Use Anxiety Control instead).*

B 100 Complex – 1 capsule, 2 times daily for 7 days or until acute stage passes.

After the acute stage passes, *use the supplement program outlined in Chapter 11.* If you use alcohol because you have anxiety, panic, or chronic pain, you are in a losing battle. When you put back in the brain the nutrients that belong there, you will heal mentally and physically. Withdrawal symptoms effect all ages, races, and incomes. Using the supplement program reduces these symptoms and is very safe. Do not turn to antidepressants such as SSRIs or tranquilizers as you are only trading one addiction for another.

> ## Alcohol Withdrawal Syndrome
> - Caused by not drinking
> - Usually short-lived lasting 3 to 7 days
> - Marked by tremors with hallucinations and grand mal seizures
> - Desperate need of B Complex vitamins, especially Thiamine
> - DTs (Delirium tremens) sometimes accompany acute withdrawal. DTs marked by memory disturbance, disorientation, confusion, and auditory and/or visual hallucinations. (Body desperately needs magnesium.)
> - Nausea and vomiting
> - Insomnia
> - Agitation
> - Anxiety
> - Sweating
> - Rapid pulse (tachycardia)
>
> Usually after four to five days, withdrawal symptoms improve greatly. However, symptoms of anxiety, insomnia, *white knuckles, dry drunks,* may persist for up for three to six months.

Alcoholics constitute a large group of potential suicidal risks, particularly older males, living alone with no family and suffering from chronic health problems. Alcohol is known to induce depression. This causes a depletion of neurotransmitters needed by the brain. Alcoholics present a number of neurological syndromes attributed to vitamin and amino acid deficiencies. Alcohol increases urinary excretion of magnesium and zinc.

Although no specific type of personality appears predisposed to drug or alcohol addiction, stress, anxiety, depression, and especially unresolved feelings seem to increase the potential. Specific personality traits may become more prominent in certain situations. The introvert may become extroverted, the gentle one violent, the sensitive one insensitive, and so on. In the early stages those with alcohol problems become more irritable, moody, and depressed when

Symptoms Of Alcohol Withdrawal
(Mild Or Early)

Behavior Changes
 Irritability
 Restlessness
 Agitation
 Hostility
 Exaggerated startle response

Sleep Disturbances
 Insomnia
 Restless sleep
 Nightmares

Impaired Cognitive Function
 Easily distracted
 Impairment of memory
 Inability to concentrate
 Impairment of judgment and other mental functions

Gastrointestinal Problems
 Appetite loss
 Nausea
 Vomiting
 Abdominal discomfort
 Diarrhea

Muscular Symptoms
 Cramps
 Weakness
 Trembling

Autonomic Imbalances
 Tachycardia or rapid heart beat >100 beats/minute
 Systolic hypertension (high blood pressure)
 Shakiness
 Fever
 Sweating or diaphoresis

not drinking. He denies that he is drinking too much, blaming his drinking on his stress, his job, or even his family.

Those with alcohol problems sees the world as close, threatening and depression producing. The alcoholic uses alcohol to solve his problems because they seem to diminish after a drink—his blood alcohol increases and the self-degenerating circuits of the brain are anesthetized. Alcoholism is not a reaction to a situation, rather it is a basic primary drive as powerful hunger that has been established by and associated with chemical alcohol. The relief from the alcohol is only a temporary lift and relief from the depression is short-lived. Alcohol is a central nervous system depressant. After the high wears off the depression can intensify. Addiction is a vicious cycle and once the behavior is established the problems continue with intensity. Alcohol shares similar properties with many hypnotic and antianxiety drugs. Alcohol serves as courage for alcoholics since it works primarily on anticipatory anxiety. Most alcoholics live in a constant state of anxiety, have sleep disturbances, sexual dysfunction, as well as multiple nonspecific medical problems.

Alcoholics have a major problem with nutritional deficiencies that, in turn, cause many major health problems. Alcohol has a direct toxic effect on the pancreas, producing acute pancreatitis and hyperglycemia which is activated by chronic drinking. Chronic pancreatitis is common in alcoholics. A number of neurological syndromes occurring in chronic alcoholics can be attributed to vitamin deficiencies. The nutritional problems of alcoholics are more complex than those found in any other single group with addiction problems.

Magnesium deficiency is a major problem associated with symptoms of anxiety, depression, muscle spasm, tremors, and chronic pain. Deficiencies occur in anyone using addictive substances as well as chronic stress syndrome.

Historically, society has taken a dim view of alcoholism. The widely accepted *treatment* has been punishment such as stoning during biblical times to the modern day *drunk tank*. Recently, alcoholism has been recognized as a disease. However, it has been classified as a personality disorder that is defined by the American

Symptoms Of Alcohol Withdrawal
(Late Or Severe)

Worsening of mild symptoms of alcohol withdrawal
Tremor
Tachycardia
Agitation
Diaphoresis
Marked startle response

Delusions
Paranoia
Mixed with and reinforced by hallucinations
Can create agitation and terror

Hallucinations
Can be visual, auditory, or tactile
Can be threatening in nature

Delirium
Changes from one hour to the next in severity and nature
Impairment of thinking
Disorientation as to time and place
Clouding of senses

Seizures
Usually generalized and nonfocal
History of prior seizure disorder not necessary
Usually occurs within 48 hours after cessation of drinking
Usually self-limiting
Always precede severe delirium, agitation, and hallucinations.

Psychiatric Association as *alcohol dependence syndrome*. Alcoholism is viewed as a psychological disease rather than a physical disease because of this classification. As such, treatment gears toward resolving it through counseling and support without ever considering the very real physiological and nutritional aspects. More and more scientists recognize alcoholism as a complex disease, not simply, a lack of moral character or will power. Many factors contribute to alcoholism—genetic, physiologic, nutritional, psychological, and social. At the Pain & Stress Center, we believe genetics and nutritional status are among the strongest influencing factors and the least appreciated in conventional treatment models for alcoholism.

If you are reading this book, you probably have some knowledge of all these statistics. You have lived with the consequences of alcohol, either through your own addiction, or the addiction of someone you love. You know first hand the pain and cost of alcohol abuse. You might also know the success rate of conventional treatment programs is not good. Commonly cited statistics for alcohol treatment programs nationwide is less than 20 percent recover after one year.

At the Pain & Stress Center we have seen that alcoholism is a biochemical disease caused and sustained by deficiencies and imbalances of neurotransmitters in the brain. We have successfully treated alcohol addiction, depression, anxiety, and A.D.D. (Attention Deficit Disorder) with nutritional therapy.

This is not a new thought nor is it unique to the Pain & Stress Center. Studies as early as 1960 show the benefits of nutrition for alcoholism. Joseph Beasley, M.D., author of *How to Defeat Alcoholism; Nutritional Guidelines for Getting Sober* says, "For the alcoholic metabolism is far stronger than free will. Diet and nutrition therapy should be part of an alcohol treatment program."

So let's begin to understand the biochemistry of alcoholism and how with proper nutrition, you greatly improve your probability of recovery.

2
Genetics

Genetics is about the characteristics or traits you inherit from your biological parents. Your genetic makeup determines what color hair and eyes you have and also determines what diseases you are susceptible to. Scientists are realizing there is a strong genetic link to alcoholism. A number of studies have shown alcoholism is four to five times more common in the biologic children of alcoholic than to nonalcoholic parents, whether or not their parent(s) raised these children. Studies done on identical twins separated at birth with one child being raised in an alcoholic family and the other in a non-alcoholic environment, found that there was no significant difference in the incidences of alcoholism between the two groups. In the studies conducted, environment didn't have any real effect on whether or not these identical twins developed alcoholism.

Studies overwhelmingly demonstrate the closer someone is genetically to an alcoholic, the more likely they are to develop the disease. The children and grandchildren of alcoholics appear to have inherited a unique biological response to alcohol. This is not a personality flaw or a lack of will power, but a genetically encoded or hardwired difference in the way they metabolize alcohol. Once alcohol is introduced to a person with this genetic encoding, craving followed by alcoholism is the most likely outcome. This genetic predisposition holds true no matter where, how, or with whom you are raised.

As this is being written, scientists are coming closer to isolating the specific genes that contribute to alcoholism. This has been a 15 year, 65 million dollar Collaborative Study on the Genetics of Alcoholism (COGA). A paper published January 14, 2004 in *Alcoholism: Clinical and Experimental Research* journal, pinpointed a specific gene on chromosome 15 that helps regulate gamma-amino butyric acid (GABA), the major inhibitory neurotransmitter in the brain and body. GABA controls the anxiety *stop* switch. Another group of researchers in this study have identified several parts of chromosome 4 that could contain genes related to alcohol metabolism and GABA receptors. Danielle Dick, psychiatry professor, Washington University School of Medicine in St. Louis and principal author of the study states: "It is important to say that these genes all influence your risk."

It is important to understand these genes only influence the risk of becoming alcoholic. Having a risk of disease not a sentence of, nor an excuse for alcoholism. It was once thought genetic traits were "cast in stone." However, when it comes to brain chemistry, we have learned gene behavior can be changed and redirected using specific amino acids and nutrients.

In April 2004 researchers using brain wave patterns established a low amplitude P3 was predictive of alcoholism and is frequently found in alcoholic parents and their young children. Later studies indicate people whose P3 is below the normal range have a much higher risk of many types of mental problems.

The genetic predisposition to alcoholism seems to manifest through an inborn difference in the way alcoholics metabolize alcohol. In 1977 a group of Harvard scientists discovered a liver enzyme named, alcohol dehydrogenase II, that processes alcohol up to 40 percent more efficiently than the usual liver enzymes. Most people do not have this enzyme, but those who do, have the ability to drink very large amounts of alcohol without becoming intoxicated, or suffering a hangover the next day.

The other end of this spectrum exists in people of Asia decent. Many Orientals have only one liver enzyme rather than the usual two for processing alcohol. Their reaction to alcohol can be either mild to becoming very sick for up to 24 hours after ingesting alcohol. These people have an inborn metabolic aversion to alcohol. There is a very low incidence of alcoholism among Oriental populations.

Studies done with the sons of alcoholics clearly demonstrate the children of alcoholics actually respond differently to alcohol. Rather than losing motor control and coherence, they actually experience less feelings of drunkenness, improved hand-eye coordination, improved muscle control and less of a stress reaction. Some researchers noted higher blood levels of acetaldehyde in the blood serum after drinking compared to nonalcoholic subjects. (We will discuss acetaldehyde in detail a little later.)

Studies using PET (positron emission tomography) scans have shown three distinct reactions to alcohol in the brain. These studies further demonstrate differing biological responses to alcohol. In some people the brain's reward system lit up when they drank; alcohol stimulates these people, and they like drinking. Others became sedated; their reward system did not become involved and these people do not like to drink. The remaining people were somewhere in between and could go either way. This demonstrates how the genes influence behavior and how important the genetic link is in the addiction process.

The brain's reward or pleasure center is part of the limbic network located in the midbrain. All animals, even lizards, have a limbic system. The limbic system is essential for survival by rewarding behaviors that enhance evolutionary adaptation. The reward system reinforces behaviors necessary for survival by giving emotional boosters that range from intense highs to satisfaction for a job well done. According to Dr. George Koob, a neuropsychopharmacologist at the Scripps Research Institute in La Jolla, California, "The reward system brings limbic information—emotional information—into the area of the brain that controls behavior." The system is usually somewhat stingy passing out wonderful sensations—what would be the motivation if we lived with constant extremes highs. For some people alcohol is a strong activator of the pleasure center. Alcohol offers escape to those with fear or situations they don't know how to handle.

James Olds discovered the brain's pleasure center in the late 1950's. He inserted a thin electrode into the primitive limbic system of rat. This electrode was wired to a bar which when pressed would stimulate the pleasure center. The rats would press the bar thousands of times an hour, foregoing food or water, until they collapsed with exhaustion.

A specially bred line of alcoholic rats showed similar behavior when presented with an opportunity to have alcohol dispensed by pressing on a bar. These rats pressed the bar fewer times per hour than the rats who had been "direct wired," partly because alcohol is less stimulating to the pleasure center than an electrical zap, but because the rats become intoxicated and unable to press the bar any longer.

As stated earlier in reference to the PET scans, in some people ingested alcohol zips to the reward center in the brain, literally lighting it up, giving the message, alcohol is good, give me more. These individuals have a faulty GABA switch in the brain. We will discuss the importance of GABA in later chapters.

> "It appears that uncontrolled craving for alcohol for certain individuals is a nutritional deficiency. The efficiency of diet supplementation in diminishing alcohol consumption has been demonstrated hundreds of times; and regardless of interpretation, the fact must be accepted."
>
> Dr. Roger Williams
> Author of *Biochemical Individuality*

3
Neurotransmitters

It was once thought the brain communicated through electrical impulses and was *hard* wired, sort of like the wiring in your house. Cells in the brain are not even physically connected, and communication between neurons (brain cells) is a complex electrochemical process involving neurotransmitters and receptor sites. Neurotransmitters are the chemical language of the brain. Neurotransmitters derive from amino acids and produced by neurons. When released, they filter across a small gap called the synapse and stimulate receptor sites of neighboring neural cells, creating a domino effect of communication. Joseph Le Doux, author of *Synaptic Self,* believes the synapses, the spaces between neurons, are the true creators of who we are; what we think, how we act, what we feel, our personality traits, preferences and beliefs. The synapse is the area where alcohol, street drugs, and all psychiatric drugs such as Prozac, Paxil,

The Synapse

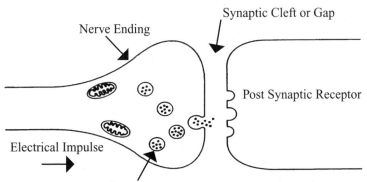

In the brain, neurotransmitters like serotonin and norepinephrine carry signals from one nerve to the next across the gap (synapse) between the two nerve cells to allow communication. Antidepressant drugs work by keeping more neurotransmitters in the synapse.

Ativan, etc. have their effects.

There are more than one hundred known neurotransmitters, but we are only concerned with just a few that alcohol seems to affect directly. Neurotransmitters are responsible for every thought and emotion we have. These chemical messengers stimulate the brain's pleasure center. Neurotransmitters are the regulators of when we feel hungry, how we respond to stress, if we are happy or sad. One group of neurotransmitters, the endorphins and enkephalins, act as our own natural painkillers. Tests have shown the brain's natural painkillers are much more potent than any drug available.

You need knowledge of the brain and how neurotransmitters function to understand the effects of alcohol, drugs, and even some foods. The brain is the body's most protected organ. Fearful of importing something harmful into itself, the brain makes almost all of its own chemicals. Further, the brain protects itself with a phenomenon known as the blood-brain barrier. Nature designed to protect the brain from water-soluble toxins. Despite all these protective measures, the brain readily imports certain plant-based components that are chemically very close to our own neurotransmitters. These pseudo-brain chemicals are what cause the grief of addiction.

When nature develops a system that works well, it uses it over and over again in all kinds of applications. It is because of this tendency of nature that humans share many genes with other animals as well as plants. Some of the chemicals found in alcohol, cocaine, nicotine, and heroin are close chemical cousins of the brain's natural neurotransmitters. These substances readily the blood-brain barrier becasue of their similar chemical structure. According to Joseph D. Beasley, M.D., author of *How To Defeat Alcoholism*, "These chemicals are capable of affecting the balance of neurotransmitters in the brain. They do this by being structurally similar to natural neurotransmitters and stimulating receptor sites. By interfering with reuptake so that more of the neurotransmitter stays in the synapse and increases stimulation; or by combining with other biochemicals to form substances which can either block reuptake or stimulate receptors (and sometimes both). If you understand how a drug works, you will understand that it interacts or mimicks a chemical that is already produced by the brain."

The over stimulation of our own brain chemicals creates the high experienced from any drug, including alcohol. If our own brain chemicals are so powerful, why aren't we high all the time? The answer is very simple—the pleasure center of the brain is stingy with these feel-good chemicals. The brain and body always strives for balance. We are not designed to live in extreme conditions *all* the time. Our mind and bodies burn out quickly with constant excess, which is what we see in alcoholics and drug addicts. If we become very frightened and have a huge adrenalin surge, as soon as it passes, you feel very weak and shaky, need to rest, and recuperate. For every action, there is an equal and opposite reaction—this physical law is one reason why after the high of alcohol or any drug passes, the crash goes so low. When the low hits, the body feels worse than it's original state and craves relief with another high.

This over-stimulation disrupts the natural balance and ultimately, causes all the trouble. When we introduce alcohol, drugs, nicotine, or even sugar into our system, you replace natural chemicals with unnatural ones. The body responds to these outside chemicals by reducing production of neurotransmitters, assuming it has enough. Alcohol, a non-nutrient (meaning it supplies calories, but not nutrition), requires a huge amount of nutrients to be metabolized, exhausting the body's supply of natural resources. When alcohol or drugs are withdrawn quickly, the brain is unable to make sufficient neurotransmitters for normal brain function. This causes an immediate insufficiency of brain chemicals making you feel awful. As the brain cries for more of the substance to feel *normal*, the chemistry of addiction becomes established.

More than 40 percent of individuals who begin drinking before age 13 will develop alcohol abuse or alcohol dependency at some time during their lifetime.

4
Alcohol's Effect on Neurotransmitters

Alcohol affects several different neurotransmitters and their receptor sites depending on the amount ingested. Each neurotransmitter has a different function, which is why responses differ as more alcohol is consumed.

GABA (Gamma Amino Butyric Acid) is an inhibitory neurotransmitter found throughout the central nervous system. GABA is called the *stop* switch as it causes brain cells to shut down, inducing a sense of calm. When the body does not have enough GABA, a person feels anxious all the time, and with a severe deficiency, they can have panic attacks. At the Pain & Stress Center we recommend supplementing GABA to reduce anxiety and panic attacks.

For some alcoholics, drinking activates the GABA *stop* switch that initially allows escape from on-going anxiety. Many alcoholics, as well as persons with a bipolar disorder, drink alcohol as a way of self-medicating anxiety.

Closely linked to the GABA receptor is the NMDA (N-methyl-D-aspartate) receptor. The NMDA receptor is responsible for firing an electrical charge through cells that create a memory pathway. While the GABA receptor is the *stop* switch, NMDA is the *go* switch. Alcohol blocks the NMDA receptor, thereby impairing memory. If you have trouble remembering events when drinking, it is because alcohol blocked the NMDA receptors so new memories couldn't be established.

Both GABA and NMDA are closely linked to the reward system. Things done while drinking become tinged with pleasurable memories, setting the stage for craving, and completing the cycle for craving. Not everyone has the same reaction to alcohol, and even those who are prone to alcoholism respond to different effects. Some are drawn to the calming effects, and others for the euphoria associated with alcohol. Why the difference? At the Pain & Stress Center, we believe the underlying cause of alcoholism comes from specific nutritional deficiencies and genetics that ultimately affect one or more of the different neurotransmitters in the brain. For example, if you are deficient in GABA, you usually have high levels of anxiety, poor concentration, and memory. You may drink for the calming effects of alcohol. Other people drink because it elevates their mood, making them feel euphoric and confident. When alcohol affects you in this way, it elevates your serotonin levels.

When serotonin is low, people are aggressive and display anger. In the experiment with the drinking rats at the Indiana University School of Medicine, the rats started off with a low serotonin level as shown by their aggressive behavior. Once the rats started drinking alcohol, they calmed down and stopped biting their neighbors. This leads scientists to believe that initially alcohol increases serotonin levels in the brain. Which makes sense, ingesting carbohydrates is known to raise serotonin levels. However, after the initial rise of serotonin, alcohol produces a rebound effect causing serotonin levels to drop significantly with continued consumption, increasing the risk for aggression and depression.

If you or someone you know drinks for alcohol's calming effects, perhaps you can relate to Cindy. Cindy, a young woman, called the Pain & Stress Center and shared her story. She was 28 years old and a mother of two children. Cindy had always been somewhat shy and suffered from on-going anxiety, but she had always managed to maintain control.

Cindy had been promoted at work and the demands of work and family were overwhelming. She began to have a drink after work to ease the stress of the day and to help her unwind. For a while this helped. But soon she was drinking every night and consuming larger amounts. With the increased intake she was now faced with *hangovers* the next day at work and her anxiety increased. She could hardly wait for five o'clock each day so she could go home and start drinking. Where alcohol once had helped her relax and feel calmer, it now consumed her, making her more and more irritable, and less able to meet the demands of her job and her family's needs.

On one especially bad day at work, when deadlines were short, and tempers even shorter, a friend told Cindy about Anxiety Control, an amino acid supplement that helped her cope with stress. Cindy began taking it and noticed an immediate difference. Not only did it relieve Cindy's anxiety, she noticed she felt a decreased need to drink.

Feeling better now, Cindy decided to take a serious look at her drinking. Her father had been an alcoholic and Cindy had always promised herself that she would not follow in his footsteps. Cindy started seeing a therapist and worked with us in developing a supplement program to address nutritional needs that supported her sobriety.

> *Once the drinking habit forms, the already low level of endorphins and enkephalins in your brain continues to decrease. Alcohol dependence now becomes increasing intense. Your need becomes a must.*

5
Alcohol Metabolism and Acetaldehyde

The metabolism of alcohol is a fairly complex process involving several different enzymes. All mammals, including humans, make a small amount of alcohol in the body as part of normal metabolism. In this process the average person makes about one ounce of alcohol per day, which is broken down in the liver by an enzyme called alcohol dehydrogenase. This enzyme also handles the alcohol ingested from alcoholic beverages.

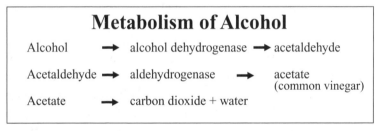

In the next step, alcohol is converted by alcohol dehydrogenase to acetaldehyde, and this substance can damage the body in several ways:

1. It can cause abnormal chemical bonds in large molecules like proteins (causing hardening of the arteries, loss of elasticity, skin wrinkling).
2. It can damage the DNA molecule (resulting in abnormal cell function).
3. Damage can also result when acetaldehyde is oxidized in the body, yielding dangerous and reactive chemical fragments called free radicals; these can cause damage to many cell structures, cancer, birth defects, atherosclerosis, and are implicated as major factors in aging.

Acetaldehyde is a very toxic chemical, and the body breaks it down by the enzyme called aldehyde dehydrogenase. The breakdown is most crucial. If the liver does not produce enough aldehyde dehydrogenase, many toxic side effects can occur, especially to the liver cells. *Normal* people who do not ingest excess alcohol have no difficulty breaking down the alcohol to acetate in their bodies. The enzyme system becomes overloaded when you ingest alcohol too quickly. Acetaldehyde and its free radical by-products from the alcohol breakdown cause most of the damage to the body and the brain, including cardiovascular disease, premature aging, liver damage, brain damage, lowered resistance to disease, alcohol addiction, etc.

In the brain an overload of acetaldehyde leads to bizarre and complicated chemical reactions. It competes with other chemical substances known as brain amines or neurotransmitters for the attention of certain enzymes. Acetaldehyde blocks the enzymes from achieving their primary duty of inhibiting the neurotransmitter activity. Addiction to alcohol might never occur if acetaldehyde stopped interfering at this point with the brain's chemical activities. The brain neurotransmitters interact with acetaldehyde to form compounds called *isoquinolines*. These compounds also release the stored neurotransmitters. The isoquinolines are very similar to the opiates, and research has suggested that they may act on the opiate receptors in the brain. The opiate receptors may contribute to the addiction of alcohol. These mischievous substances trigger the alcoholic to drink more and more to counter the painful effects of the increasing buildup of acetaldehyde.

Recently, scientists have discovered that many alcoholics have a metabolic defect which causes them to have twice as much of the toxic acetaldehyde in their bloodstream after a drink as normal people. This is enough to set the vicious cycle into motion. Acetaldehyde made by the liver makes the drinker feel bad. He drinks more alcohol; this makes him feel better, and helps to protect him from the acetaldehyde poison—until the liver produces more acetaldehyde out of the additional alcohol, so he continues to drink.

Researchers continue to look for the *one cause of alcoholism*. But all research has concluded that there is no one factor; studies have shown that a number of physiological differences exist between the nonalcoholic and the alcoholic. Physiology determines whether one person becomes alcoholic and another does not. The alcoholic's body—his hormones, enzymes, genes, and brain chemistry—all work jointly to cause his abnormal reaction to alcohol. Of course, psychological, family history, and social factors certainly influence the alcoholic's drinking habits and behavior.

Alcoholism and nutrition are interrelated and intertwined on many levels:

1. *Ethyl alcohol, or ethanol, itself contains nutrients; however, it also changes the balance of other nutrients in the diet and may disperse them as well.*
2. *The absorption and digestion of many nutrients is affected by the ingestion of ethanol; it may alter dietary requirements.*
3. *In addiction, nutritional alterations may affect the metabolism of alcohol in the body.*
4. *Chronic alcohol consumption may cause temporary or permanent damage to many organs—the liver, brain, heart, and bone marrow. The effects may be modified by nutritional factors such as dietary intake of protein, fat, and vitamins.*
5. *Organ damage may yield changes in nutrient metabolism. The organ most affected is the liver. The liver plays an important role in metabolism and is frequently altered with alcohol ingestion.*

If your liver is constantly flooded with alcohol, it adapts by establishing an additional system for processing alcohol called the microsomal ethanol oxidizing system, or MEOS. The MEOS increases your liver's ability to process alcohol, but the trade off is an increased production of acetaldehyde. Since the MEOS allows faster processing of alcohol, the individual drinks more with less obvious effects—this is known as tolerance. While on the surface it seems like an ideal arrangement, the down side is the MEOS does not speed up the elimination of highly toxic acetaldehyde. The increased actaldehyde levels begin to kill off the very liver cells needed to eliminate it leading to cirrhosis.

Once the MEOS is established it becomes the driving force behind alcohol consumption. The MEOS requires more alcohol to keep it functioning, this creates a biological need for alcohol followed by addiction and alcohol craving. The amount of alcohol required to feel normal increases as tolerance increases. And to make matters worse, acetaldehyde accumulates, causing cellular damage and adaptations in other systems.

Acetaldehyde binds with many other compounds, including the neurotransmitters known as the catecholamines. When this happens the resulting compounds closely resemble the body's naturally occurring opiates, the endorphins and enkephalins. The body sees these pseudo-neurotransmitters and assumes it has plenty and slows down or stops production of endorphins. Withdrawal symptoms occur when the alcoholic stops drinking and the artificial neurochemicals disappear; the brain is unable to produce endorphins quickly enough to compensate. Alcohol disrupts the production of many neurotransmitters, affecting appetite, sleep, sexual drive, and every other regulatory function of the brain. Functionally, the alcoholic experiences a process very similar to heroin addiction.

If you start drinking before age 14, you are twelve times more likely to be injured while under the influence sometime in your lifetime.

6
Nutrition and Alcoholism

Addressing the nutritional needs of the alcoholic is absolutely necessary for the successful treatment of this disease. Treatment from a strictly psychological standpoint is like telling a diabetic to attend twelve-step meetings to control their disease. It's just not going to work. Failure to address the nutritional needs of the recovering alcoholic is one of the primary reasons for the dismal statistics of recovery programs. With proper nutrition, recovery from alcoholism is not a white-knuckle experience where extreme will power is needed. When the correct vitamins, minerals, amino acids and essential fatty acids are taken the need for alcohol diminishes naturally.

Your body is an amazing chemical factory—working 24/7 to keep you healthy and functioning. For example, new blood cells are manufactured at the rate of 2.4 million each second to just replace the worn-out blood cells. In a perfect world, food would be the only source needed for vitamins, minerals, and amino acids that allows this awesome chemical factory to keep functioning. Realistically in today's, high stress, polluted world, supplementation is essential. The foods you eat give you the energy to live, work, and allows for the growth and regeneration of cells. Your very health and happiness is dependant on the nutritional fuel you feed your body.

Identifying the cause of malnutrition in alcoholism is not a simple matter. Certain groups of alcoholics may have an inadequate nutrient intake, but a major factor is the primary toxic effect of ethanol on the gastrointestinal tract, pancreas, liver, bone marrow, and other tissues such as the heart. Research data by Rubin and Lieber in 1974 suggested that a nutritious diet could not and will not prevent the development of alcoholic liver disease.

Alcoholic beverages provide mainly calories that are derived

Factors Leading To Malnutrition In Alcoholism

1. **Decreased or sporadic food ingestion**
   Intoxication
   Poverty and economic factors
   Abnormal appetite
   Anorexia
   Mental illness/disease

2. **Increased nutrient losses**
   Urinary
   Toxic effects of alcohol on the kidneys
   Fecal
   a) Malabsorption due to GI effects of alcohol
   b) Maldigestion due to inflamed pancreas

3. **Reduced or deficient nutrient stores**
   Decreased uptake of nutrients
   Alcoholic hepatitis
   Cirrhosis (inflammation of liver)
   Reduced nutrient intake
   Increased inactivation of vitamins and nutrients

4. **Impaired nutrient utilization due to defective metabolism**
   Alcoholic liver disease
   Toxic effects of alcohol on bone marrow

from their ethanol content. A pint of 86 proof liquor supplies about half the normal daily calories required by an adult, but these alcoholic calories are utterly empty of other nutrients. Ethanol does not even provide caloric food value equal to carbohydrates. If alcohol consumption is heavy and the drinker limits his food intake, he worsens his already severe vitamin and nutrient deficiencies. Conversely, if he does not reduce his food intake, many of the extra ethanol calories are converted to fat, causing high serum triglyceride and cholesterol levels and obesity.

Alcohol/Drug-Induced Nutritional Deficiencies

Vitamins Depleted
Folic acid
Thiamine
Niacin
Riboflavin
Ascorbic acid (Vitamin C)
Vitamin B6
Vitamin B12

Mineral Depleted
Calcium
Magnesium
Zinc

Each vitamin and mineral performs many different functions. Deficiencies affect your health in profound ways. For example, magnesium alone is responsible for over 350 different enzymatic actions in the body. When deficiencies exist, your body is unable to function properly. The absence of even one nutrient has serious physical and mental consequences. Examples of the importance of single nutrients are seen in the history of scurvy caused by Vitamin C deficiency and pellagra, a deficiency of niacin. Although we don't hear much about the incidence of those diseases today, many people are experiencing diseases that stem from nutritional insufficiency. The increase of heart disease, depression, addiction, anxiety, and A.D.D. seen in the United States can be directly correlated to the decrease in the nutritional quality of the Standard American diet.

Quoting Joseph D. Beasley, M.D., "Malnutrition is more than just the absence of food; it is the absence of nutrients in the right amounts and correct balance." Although we live in a country where an abundance of food exists, today's fast food, highly processed and sugar coated diets make us a society of malnourished, obese people. This statement is even truer of the alcoholic.

Alcohol is a negative nutrient. Alcohol does not provide any of nutrient value, and it requires stored nutrients for its metabolism. An alcoholic often consumes 50 percent or more of their daily calories in alcohol with the remaining calories often provided by junk foods—chips, chocolate, sweets, and other quick energy foods. These foods provide empty calories as well leaving the alcoholic in a seriously malnourished state.

Chronic drinking causes severe nutritional deficiencies that in turn, causes many major health problems. Alcohol has a direct toxic effect on the pancreas producing acute pancreatitis, and hypoglycemia that is activated by chronic drinking. A number of neurological syndromes occurring in chronic drinkers can be attributed to vitamin and mineral deficiencies. Just to name a few, these include: Wernicke's-Korsakoff's syndrome, peripheral neuropathy, Morel's carotid sclerosis, and cellular degeneration. Alcoholics have alterations in the metabolism of the B vitamins. Commonly, chronic drinking decreases vitamin B1 (thiamine), B3 (niacin), B6 (pyridoxine), B12, B15, and folic acid. Anemias occur with deficiencies of folic acid or B6, while deficiencies of niacin or thiamine cause neurological symptoms.

Anxiety, depression, muscle spasms, tremors, and chronic pain show up in alcoholics due to magnesium deficiencies, common among chronic drinkers. Deficiencies, as well as chronic stress syndrome, occur in anyone using addictive substances.

Acute and chronic consumption of alcohol may markedly alter digestion and gastrointestinal absorption. Alcohol-induced changes in digestion and absorption may yield deficiencies or augment deficiencies arising from other causes.

Alcohol ingestion alters the metabolism of the fat-soluble vitamins. In alcoholics with cirrhosis, vitamin A deficiencies may occur due to poor absorption, impaired liver storage of vitamin A, or simply, too much alcohol in the body competing in the liver. Vitamin D may be depleted through dietary insufficiency. Vitamin K deficiency in the alcoholic may manifest itself as a bleeding disorder related to the liver's failure to make clotting factors.

Chronic alcohol consumption causes mineral deficiencies, especially calcium, magnesium and zinc. Alcohol increases the excretion of these minerals via the kidneys. Delirium tremors result from magnesium deficiency and causes these *symptoms of horror.* Low levels of calcium occur as a result of increased excretion of calcium in the urine over a period of years. This often leads to osteoporosis.

Deficiencies of essential fatty acids are common among alcoholics. Low levels of DHA (docosahexaenoic acid) and EPA (Eicosapentaenoic acid) contribute to excessive inflammation that causes many chronic diseases such as heart disease, high blood pressure, diabetes, cancer, and Alzheimer's disease. Fatty acids compose sixty percent of the brain. When DHA and EPA levels are low, the brain substitutes with inferior fats leading to poor function. This can manifest as depression, Attention Deficit Disorder, addictions, and bipolar disorder.

A protein deficiency usually exists due to malnutrition. For full recovery, alcoholics need to address the wide range of deficiencies caused by drinking. Using nutritional supplements is imperative as well as eating an improved diet. When these steps are taken, recovery is such a joy.

> *Alcohol causes you to produce chemicals called tetrahydroisoquinolines (TIQs) that are similar to morphine and heroin. As they fill the enkephalin receptors, you experience an unnatural euphoria reducing the output of natural endorphins and enkephalins. Large amounts of alcohol over many years cause a permanent, urgent need for alcohol and the craving for more.*

7
Hypoglycemia, The Sugar Connection

Blood sugar or glucose is the fuel that runs your body. It is the primary fuel for the brain—the brain cannot function for more than one minute without a constant supply of glucose. However too much blood sugar is harmful as well. The body regulates blood sugar levels through the hormone insulin, which acts as an escort, moving glucose out of the blood stream and into the cells. When there is more glucose than the cells can use, insulin stores excess sugar as fat.

Symptoms of Low Blood Sugar

- Anxiety
- Fatigue
- Nervousness
- Ravenous hunger
- Headaches
- Restlessness
- Dizziness
- Insomnia
- Sweet or alcohol cravings
- Heart palpitations
- Depression
- Drowsiness

The body obtains sugar from dietary carbohydrates like bread, potatoes, pasta, corn and rice; and of course the obvious sugar contained in candy, soda, cakes, and cookies. What many people don't realize is that potatoes, rice, white bread and pasta convert very quickly to sugar in the system. Although they don't taste sweet like sugar they are no different than eating a donut in terms of what they do to blood sugar levels. Most of the vital nutrients have been stripped from white bread and white rice, leaving them with little, if any, nutritional value.

Carbohydrates are classified as either simple or complex based on the number of molecules strung together. The number of molecules in a carbohydrate string will determine how quickly they are digested and absorbed into the blood stream. Complex carbohydrates can contain over one hundred molecules in a single string. They digest more slowly supplying the body with a steady stream of glucose and does not trigger excessive insulin release.

Simple sugars contain one or two molecules giving them quick entry into the blood stream. Alcohol is a carbohydrate—a very fast acting sugar that does not have to go through the process of digestion to be absorbed. Diets high in simple sugars increase blood sugar levels too high too quickly. This causes the pancreas to release large amounts of insulin causing a quick drop in blood sugar resulting in hypoglycemia or low blood sugar. The body's response to this emergency (remember the brain can't live for more than one minute without blood sugar) is to crave more sugar starting the process all over again. These wildly vacillating blood sugars play havoc on mood and energy levels, but for alcoholics, it increases their cravings. Many alcoholics suffer from hypoglycemia due to alcohol consumption, irregular eating habits, and poor diets filled with sugar-laden foods.

There are many names for the sweet stuff known as sugar. This list will make you aware of what to look for on package labels.

Sugar By It's Many Names

- Sucrose
- High-fructose corn syrup
- Corn sugar
- Dextrose
- Glucose
- Fructose
- Maltose
- Honey
- Molasses
- Lactose
- Mannitol
- Sorbital
- Xylitol

To avoid hypoglycemic episodes, you want to avoid any product that has any one of these listed in the first four ingredients. Food manufacturers disguise sugar in a product by using several different types of sugar. For example, a popular cracker lists its ingredients as enriched flour, partially hydrogenated oil, sugar, salt, leavening, high fructose corn syrup. By dividing the sugar into three different kinds, they make it appear that the product contains less sugar than it actually does. Ketchup, mayonnaise, mustard, salad dressing, peanut butter, and canned/bottled fruit juice all contain sugar and should be avoided. *Read product labels so you know what you are ingesting.*

To recover successfully from alcoholism, it is imperative to correct the diet and stop the occurrences of hypoglycemia. The key to blood sugar control is in what we eat and drink. Limit your intake of sugar and carbohydrates. The first step is to eat a diet that contains quality protein, lots of fresh vegetables, and smaller amounts of fruits and carbohydrates like bread, pasta, rice and corn. Fats are also an essential part of a healthy diet. We recommend using real butter and olive or canola oil.

Don't skip meals. This sends your blood sugar plummeting, and you will be looking for a quick sugar fix. The amino acids, glutamine and glycine, help stop sugar craving. Glycine has a wonderful sweet taste and can be used as a sweetener in herbal teas or sprinkled over fruit for an added sweet taste. Glutamine can serve as an alternative fuel source for the brain during a low blood sugar episode. Supplementing with chromium picolinate helps to balance blood sugar and reduce cravings as well. Chromium is important for fat distribution and regulation of cholesterol.

NOTE: If you cannot control you sugar intake now, use Gymnema Sylvestre, an herb, that blocks sugar uptake. Use one Gymnema Sylvestre 30 minutes before each meal. Later, take on your sugar addiction.

Psychological instability does not cause alcoholism. Alcoholism causes stress. It puts you out of control of your life. This makes everything hard and more complex.

8
Candida

There are more than 400 different single celled organisms, primarily bacteria and yeast that reside in your gut. Some of these are considered *good* or beneficial. Others are not so good, especially when they become the predominant organism. This intestinal flora, as it's called, has a symbiotic relationship with you; they play a vital role in your digestion as well as manufacturing chemicals that aid in your immune defense. Ideally, a delicate balance is maintained between these different organisms. But certain conditions such as taking antibiotics, alcoholism, diets high in sugar, or taking medications like Prednisone or birth control pills disrupt this balance causing an overgrowth of the yeast candida albicans. According to Sherry Rogers, M.D., overgrowth of candida could cause over one hundred health related symptoms.

Yeast lives on sugar. Diets high in carbohydrate (sugar) give them a dietary edge, allowing them to flourish. Since alcohol is a fast-acting carbohydrate, it is common for alcoholics to have yeast overgrowth.

Yeast overgrowth creates a condition known as the auto-brewery syndrome. A natural by-product of the yeast metabolism is acetaldehyde. With acetaldehyde, the yeast makes alcohol-like compounds. People with this syndrome actually produce enough alcohol to test just below the legal limits for driving a car when tested with a breath-a-lyzer. Acetaldehyde stimulates the chemistry behind alcohol craving so it is imperative to treat yeast overgrowth actively. Just quitting drinking does not make these nasty bugs go away.

At the Pain & Stress Center we use a product called Candex to treat yeast problems. Candex along with a candida suppressing diet will get this potential stumbling block under control. You must eliminate all carbohydrates in your diet for several months so you can get the yeast under control.

9
Amino Acids and Nutrients
The Keys to Recovery

Amino acid supplements have a positive effect on people suffering from addictions, whether the addiction is to alcohol, cocaine, marijuana, or prescribed medications for anxiety, pain or depression. The use of alcohol or a psychoactive drug alters and depletes the brain of naturally occurring neurotransmitters that allow us to think, make decisions, and enjoy life.

Amino acids are the building blocks of protein. If you remove all the water and fat from the body, *seventy-five (75) percent* of what is left is protein, or in it's most simple form, *amino acids*. There are nearly 40,000 distinct proteins found in the body, and they are made from only 22 amino acids called the proteogenic amino acids.

Some of these amino acids are converted into brain chemicals called neurotransmitters. Neurotransmitters control how we feel, our moods, and how well our memory functions. When neurotransmitter levels become low or out of balance, symptoms of depression, anxiety, Attention Deficit Disorder (A.D.D.), and alcohol craving manifest. Correcting the balance with amino acid supplementation has the power to cure the problem. Using nutritional supplements does not mask symptoms in the way drugs do. Using amino acid or orthomoleuclar therapy corrects the basic problem allowing for a return to optimal function.

The concept of using amino acids to treat alcoholism and mental disorders is not new. At the Pain & Stress Center, we have used amino acid therapy successfully to treat anxiety, depression, A.D.D., pain and alcoholism for over 20 years. The use of nutrition to treat these disorders is not some alternative medicine hocus-pocus, but is grounded in solid science. Linus Pauling, Nobel Prize Laureate in 1954, coined the word *orthomolecular* to describe the process of establishing the right molecules in the brain by varying the concentrations of substances normally present and required for optimum health. In other words, putting back in the brain what belongs there.

Dr. Carl Pfeiffer, founder of the Princeton BioCenter, and author of *Nutrition and Mental Illness,* offers us Pfeiffer's Law:

> "We have found that if a drug can be found to do the job of medical healing, a nutrient can be found to do the same job. When we understand how a drug works, we can imitate its action with one of the nutrients. For example, antidepressants usually enhance the effect of serotonin and epinephrine. We now know that if we give the amino acids, tryptophan or tyrosine, the body can synthesize these neurotransmitters, thereby achieving the same effect. Nutrients have fewer, milder side effects, and the challenge of the future is to replace or sometimes combine drugs with the natural healers called nutrients."

As Pfeiffer's Law infers, specific amino acids affect the levels of neurotransmitters in the brain. Alcoholism severely depletes neurotransmitters. Low levels of neurotransmitters increases the need for more alcohol in order to feel normal. This is a vicious cycle. Healing begins with amino acids.

10
What Amino Acids Do and Why You Need Them

Amino acids are protein substances your body uses to make the brain chemicals called neurotransmitters. Low levels of the neurotransmitters—serotonin, dopamine, endorphins, and GABA often precede alcoholism. If levels weren't low before alcoholism begins, they are once the alcoholism has started.

Joseph Beasley M.D. documented alcohol reduces neurotransmitters such as dopamine and serotonin. GABA is the anxiety stop switch and modulates the alcohol craving while the endorphins are the body's natural painkillers.

Initially, most alcoholics drink to boost one or more of these neurotransmitters to experience a different state of emotional being—euphoric, more self-confident, a heightened state of enjoyment or calm. Alcohol has these effects because it interacts with our own brain chemistry neurotransmitters. While alcohol increase neurotransmitter levels for a short time, it actually uses up stores of these *feel good* chemicals, leaving increasingly lower and lower levels. This perpetuates the craving for alcohol. The amino acids tryptophan, tyrosine, GABA and DLPA are responsible for increasing the primary neurotransmitters, serotonin, dopamine, and endorphins. Nutritional supplementation is the key to restoring the brain chemistry and improving negative behavior.

Serotonin and 5-HTP

Serotonin is one of the *feel good* neurotransmitters. Adequate serotonin is vital to emotional health because it mediates both anxiety and depression. People with low serotonin levels have a wide range of symptoms from irritability, anger, aggressive behavior, anxiety, panic, depression, chronic pain, alcoholism, and insomnia. These are just a few of the perplexing manifestations seen with low serotonin. When serotonin levels are balanced, you feel calm and confident, and have a positive outlook on life.

Serotonin deficiency is by far the most prevalent neurotransmitter deficiency experienced by the world's population. Just look at the enormous sales of serotonin-enhancing drugs SSRIs (Selective Serotonin Reuptake Inhibitor) such as Prozac, Paxil, Zoloft, and Lexapro. Although these drugs do increase serotonin levels, they do it in an artificial way that is ultimately unhealthy and leads to further depletion of serotonin. The SSRIs also have a number of side effects that make them an undesirable choice.

The brain manufactures serotonin in a three-step process starting with the essential amino acid, tryptophan. Tryptophan is converted to 5-HTP (5-hydroxytryptophan), which in turn is converted to serotonin. In order for tryptophan to enter the brain and convert to serotonin, it must cross the blood-brain barrier by specific carrier molecules. This process itself can be the reason for low serotonin levels. We tend to derive less tryptophan from our diets than other amino acids. All the amino acids compete for entrance to the brain. The smaller amounts of tryptophan make it less likely to enter, promoting a serotonin deficiency.

Tryptophan → 5-HTP → Serotonin

Tryptophan was removed from sale in 1989 and became available by prescription only. The FDA removed tryptophan because of a contaminated batch that caused EMS (eosinophilia-myalgia syndrome). Thirty-eight people died from this contaminated batch. Tryptophan, itself, is *very safe and was not the cause of EMS,* but rather the contamination was. When tryptophan became unavailable, researchers discovered 5-HTP that is derived from Griffonia seeds, a member of the legume or bean family. 5-HTP is one metabolic step closer to serotonin, and as an additional bonus it does not require a carrier molecule to enter the brain making it more available for conversion to serotonin.

Adequate serotonin is vital for proper sleep. Your brain uses serotonin to manufacture melatonin, your body's most powerful sleep chemical. Research studies demonstrates that supplementing with 5-HTP significantly increases melatonin levels. Taking Sleep Link, a balanced sleep formula containing 5-HTP, 30 minutes before bedtime helps prevent insomnia.

Serotonin and dopamine work together as master controllers of all the neurotransmitters. For some alcoholics, alcohol temporarily increases serotonin levels making them feel calm, relaxed and happy. Temporary is the key word here. After the initial rise serotonin levels plummet leaving the drinker anxious. Drinking is not the answer to a happier life. Increasing serotonin levels naturally with 5-HTP has lasting effects.

Note: if you are taking Selective Serotonin Reuptake Inhibitors (SSRIs) or MAOI antidepressant medications, do not take 5-HTP.

Dopamine and Tyrosine

Tyrosine is the stress amino acid and the precursor for the neurotransmitters, dopamine, norepinephrine, and adrenaline. These three neurotransmitters are known as catecholamines. When you have sufficient levels of these important neurotransmitters, you feel energized and alert. These neurotransmitters provides you with feelings of excitement and enthusiasm for life. When levels are low, you feel depressed and have difficulty with concentration and focus.

Tyrosine → Dopa →Dopamine → Norepinephrine

Dopamine is known as one of the feel good chemical in the brain. Dopamine brain cell bodies are located in the brain stem. Dopamine release in the prefrontal cortex facilitates GABA's inhibition, lowering anxiety and stress. Craving begins when brain chemicals, dopamine and serotonin drop, then addictive behavior causes you to crave a substance such as alcohol for relief. The alcoholic wants relief from stress and his logic tells him to drink more.

If you need stimulants (coffee, nicotine, and chocolate) to enjoy life and stay focused, you need tyrosine. For some people alcohol feels stimulating rather than sedating. For those people alcohol raises dopamine levels and it is imperative to take tyrosine to fully recover.

Studies have shown supplementing with tyrosine dramatically increase the levels of catecholamines. Other studies have found tyrosine relieves stress, depression, and increases concentration. We have seen these same results time and time again at the Pain & Stress Center with depressed patients as well as those with A.D.D.

Note: Do not take tyrosine if you are taking MAO antidepressants, or suffer from cirrhosis, melanoma, migraine headaches, have had cancer, or if you are schizophrenic.

GABA

GABA (Gamma Amino Butyric Acid) is the major inhibitory neurotransmitter. GABA works to slow down excitatory messages keeping you from feeling overwhelmed and anxious. When your GABA levels are high, you feel relaxed and calm. GABA is essential for brain metabolism and function.

Many alcoholics drink because of alcohol's calming effects. Alcohol activates the GABA receptor sites in the brain. But the calm achieved with alcohol is short-lived as the effects of the alcohol wears off, anxiety returns with a vengeance. Tranquilizers, like Valium and Librium, and benzodiazepines, like Xanax, Klonopin and Ativan, stimulate GABA receptors. But these drugs are very addictive and like alcohol, they become the cause of ongoing anxiety. Supplementing with GABA stops anxiety in its tracks. Some research indicates GABA helps stop cravings for alcohol. However, taking too much GABA at one time cause symptoms of tingling lips or extremities, rapid heartbeat, shortness of breath, flushing, nausea, and increased anxiety. If that happens drink 2 glasses of water, and eat a couple of soda crackers. The effect will pass quickly.

Endorphins and DLPA

Endorphins are the body's natural morphine-like substance. When endorphins are plentiful, life feels absolutely wonderful. Little things, like your favorite song, a sunrise, or a hot cup of tea are delightful. If endorphins are low, you are overly sensitive to pain, whether physical or emotional. You cry easily. Life is flat, and there is just no pleasure in any activity of life.

Recent research documents that genetically predisposed individuals have a low production of endorphins. This produces a craving for alcohol. If you are one of these individuals, drinking creates a greater deficiency that quickly places alcohol in control.

Stress, anxiety, depression, and unresolved issues all lead to a reduction of vital endorphins. This is why the brain must be fed daily and in specific amounts to be chemically balanced and able to deal with a stressful lifestyle. If alcohol consumption makes you feel euphoric and uplifted, it affects your endorphins. When alcohol is stopped, the alcoholic is left with a painful experience of life—bereft of pleasure, comfort, or joy.

The amino acid, DLPA, is the natural way to boost endorphin levels. DLPA works by preventing the breakdown of the endorphins in the brain so they are able to work longer. DLPA is also responsible for production of PEA (phenylethylamine), an energizing brain chemical, that has a structural resemblance to amphetamines. PEA is believed to be the chemical most responsible for feelings of euphoria. Low PEA levels are associated with depression.

Warning: People with PKU (Phenylketonuria), high blood pressure, or anyone taking MAO inhibitors or tricyclic antidepressants, or have a history of melanoma or cancer should not supplement with DLPA.

Glutamine

Glutamine is one of the most important supplements for

the recovering alcoholic. Not only is it an essential nutrient for healing the digestive tract, it stops alcohol craving immediatly.

Dr. Roger Williams, pioneer in glutamine research, found that 3,000 to 4,000 milligrams (mg) of glutamine daily stops the craving for alcohol as well as the craving for sweets. Glutamine is tasteless. You can open a 500 mg capsule and dissolve directly in your mouth to stop a sudden alcohol craving.

Glutamine is the third most abundant amino acid in the blood and brain and performs many important functions that are critical for the recovering alcoholic. Glutamine strengthens the immune system by supporting the multiplication of selected white blood cells that boosts the body's defense system. Glutamine aids other immune cells in killing bacteria and healing wounds.

Glutamine helps to maintain and support production of glutathione, an important antioxidant found in every cell of the body.

Alcohol consumption is very damaging to the entire digestive system. This further depletes the alcoholic's nutritional status. There is an old saying, *you are what you eat.* However, a more accurate statement is, *you are what you absorb.* A damaged and inflamed digestive tract must heal before your body can correctly digest and absorb nutrients. Once again, glutamine comes to the rescue.

Scientists at the National Institute of Health (NIH) in 1970 found glutamine to be the most important nutrient for the intestinal tract. Glutamine is the main nutrient needed for intestinal repair. During times of illness, the body uses more glutamine to help tissue repair in the kidneys, intestines, and liver. Glutamine also supports the pancreas, another organ damaged by alcohol. Japanese researchers found glutamine helps stomach ulcers heal.

BCAAs (Branched Chain Amino Acids)

The essential amino acids, leucine, isoleucine, and valine are called the branched-chain amino acids. These three amino acids are similar in structure, but have different metabolic routes. They should always be taken together and not singularly, as the ingestion of only one of BCAA decreases plasma levels of the other two.

Studies on people with alcoholic cirrhosis demonstrated benefits of consuming the branched chain amino acids as they enhance protein synthesis in the liver and muscle cells.

Super Balanced Neurotransmitter Complex (SBNC)

The brain is the hungriest organ in the body. Despite its small size, the brain uses 50% of circulating blood glucose and 20% of all inhaled oxygen. When nutritional status is poor as in alcoholism, the brain is greatly affected. Super Balanced Neurotransmitter Complex (SBNC) feeds the brain needed nutrients to maintain the optimal balance of neurotransmitters. It is critical that all the major neurotransmitters are provided daily and in sufficient amounts for the brain to be chemically balanced.

T-L Vite

Your body needs a multiple Vitamin and mineral supplement to provide a solid foundation for healing. Vitamins and minerals act as coenzymes; working with enzymes, they support all the vital functions your body performs constantly to keep you healthy.

Vitamin C

Vitamin C is a powerful antioxidant. The body requires Vitamin C for at least 300 metabolic functions in the body including tissue growth and repair, adrenal gland function, and healthy gums. It aids in the production of anti-stress hormones and supports healthy immune function. Other needs for Vitamin C are for the metabolism of folic acid, tyrosine, and phenylalanine.

As early as 1958 research showed that Vitamin C helped in detoxification of drug addicts. In 1977 researchers Alfred Libby and Irwin W. Stone published a study of the effect of Vitamin C on human drug addicts. They gave twenty-five to eighty-five grams of Vitamin C intravenously daily to heroin addicts. No withdrawal symptoms developed.

Libby found Vitamin C has the same effect on alcoholics. In 1985 Libby patented his method of detoxifying alcoholics and drug addicts with a combination of Vitamin C, calcium, magnesium, and thiamine. Many nutritionally oriented practitioners use Libby's method to detoxify patients from alcohol.

Taking megadoses of Vitamin C by mouth helps reduce cravings for alcohol as well as lessening withdrawal symptoms. At the Pain & Stress Center, we use a type of Vitamin C called Ester C. Ester C has a neutral pH so it is easier on the stomach. Studies show Ester C enters the bloodstream twice as fast and penetrates the cells more efficiently than ordinary C (ascorbic acid).

B Complex

The eleven different B Vitamins are important for the health of the nerves, skin, eyes, hair, liver, mouth, and proper brain function. B Vitamins help restore endorphin function and regenerate damaged nerves. Taking high amounts of one B Vitamin without supplementing the whole complex as a foundation causes an imbalance in the other B Vitamins.

Commonly, alcoholics are deficient in one or more of the B Vitamins. A deficiency of thiamine (Vitamin B-1) is responsible for Wernicke-Korsakoff syndrome, an irreversible brain deterioration that occurs in the later stages of alcoholism. Alcohol blocks the absorption of this Vitamin B1 (Thiamine).

Several studies done with rats have shown they become alcoholic just by removing the B Vitamins from their diet. When the B Vitamins are replaced, these rats will no longer drink alcohol preferring water, instead.

Much research has been done on the positive benefits of niacin supplementation for alcoholics. Russell Smith, M.D. did several studies of the long-term effect of niacin supplementation in alcoholics. Dr. Smith showed with niacin supplementation the cravings for alcohol were reduced, feeling of well-being increased, and moods stabilized.

The nutritional program we suggest requires supplementing with high levels of amino acids. The body requires sufficient levels of B-6 in order to metabolize amino acids.

Essential Fatty Acids

Essential fatty acids (EFA's) refer to fats that must be provided by the diet. Research in the past several years indicates low levels of the omega-3 essential fatty acids, DHA (docosahexaenoic acid) and EPA (eicosapentaenoic acid), are the underlying cause of most of the chronic diseases seen today. As with most nutrients, alcoholics are usually deficient in these fats.

Fats are either saturated, which is seen in solid fats like butter and lard, or unsaturated, like corn or canola oil. There are also oils that have been modified by the addition of hydrogen to make them solid; shortening, and margarine are two such oils. These fats are called trans fatty acids. Once these trans fatty substitutes were thought to be a healthy substitution for naturally saturated fats. But the trans fatty acid products pose major health risks to the heart and brain.

Fatty Acids

Omega-6 Fatty Acids:	Omega-3 Fatty Acids:
Linoleic acid (LA)	Alpha-linolenic acid (ALA)
Gamma-linolenic acid (GLA)	Eicosapentaenoic acid (EPA)
Arachidonic acid (AA)	Docosahexaenoic acid (DHA)

Fatty acids are categorized by an omega designation. The omega-6 and omega-3 oils are what we are concerned with in brain function and immune health. Linoleic acid (LA) and alpha-linolenic acid (ALA) are the precursors, or parent fatty acids for all the others. The chart below shows the designation of the different fatty acids.

The omega-3 and 6 fatty acids provide the raw materials for the inflammation control components of our immune system. Inflammation promoting chemicals are produced from the omega-6 fatty acids, most specifically, arachidonic acid. The omega-3 fatty acids, EPA and DHA, are anti-inflammatory in nature. Inflammation is an important component of our immune system. If you are unable to mount an inflammatory response to certain conditions, you die. However, inflammation, even in a life-threatening situation, is not meant to continue indefinitely. Once a wound or injury heals anti-inflammatory chemicals come into play and stop the inflammation. But when we are deficient in the anti-inflammatory omega-3 oils, inflammation continues causing tissue destruction. Scientists are now saying ongoing inflammation is the cause of every major disease seen today.

The key to fatty acid health is balance. Our ancestors consumed diets high in both omega-6 fats (seeds and nuts) and omega-3s (plants and game). Scientists estimate our ancestors consumption of these fatty acids was in a ratio of 1:1 to a maximum of 4:1. Today's diet provides too many omega-6 fatty acids. The representative ratio is as high as 20 or 30:1. Dr. Donald Rudin, author of *The Omega-3 Phenomenon*, estimates we have reduced our omega-3 fatty acid consumption by eighty percent compared to our ancestors. This decrease in omega-3 fatty acids directly correlates to the rise in depression, attention deficit disorder (ADD), and bipolar disorders.

The dietary imbalance seen today greatly impacts brain function. Sixty percent of our brain is composed of fat. Of that, nearly one third are polyunsaturated and must come from the essential fatty acids, linoleic acid and alpha-linolenic acid. However, little of the parent EFAs are seen in the brain. It is arachidonic acid (AA), an omega-6 EFA, and docosahexaenoic acid (DHA), an omega-3 EFA that the brain prefers.

The body can produce DHA from the essential fatty acid, alpha-linolenic acid (ALA). Researchers tell us that at best, only about fifteen percent of consumed ALA converts to DHA. Diets high in omega-6 EFAs and trans-fatty acids prevent this conversion from happening at all. You can obtain DHA directly from cold-water fish such as salmon, mackerel, herring, sardines, and anchovies, or from fish oil supplements.

DHA plays a critical role in parts of the brain that requires a high degree of electrical activity. One such area is the synapse, the microscopic gap between neurons that allows communication to occur between nerves with neurotransmitters. Low or insufficient levels of DHA impact neurotransmitter function leading to depression, anxiety, or ADD. Other areas of high DHA concentration are the photoreceptors of the retina, the mitochondria of nerve cells, and the cerebral cortex, the outer layer of the brain. If DHA is not present in adequate amounts, the brain is forced to use inferior oils for this vital work.

DHA is essential for proper brain functioning. Deficiencies of total omega-3 fatty acids and lower omega-3 to omega-6 ratio are found in patients with Alzheimer's disease, other dementias, and in cognitive impairment associated with aging.

DHA levels have a direct effect on mood. Historically, cultures where fish is eaten regularly have low levels of depression. Julia Ross, M.A., author of the *The Mood Cure* says, "Omega-3 essential fatty acids are a spectacular good-mood food." Studies show supplementing with DHA raises dopamine levels by forty percent.

Note of Caution about DHA and Fish Oils: Do not use fish oils if you are taking a anticoagulant (blood thinner) such as Coumadin. Use a product called ProDHA for supplementing DHA. ProDHA is a pharmaceutical grade, molecularly distilled omega-3 fish oil that is pure without mercury. This is very important as many fish and their oils often contain high levels of mercury, a heavy metal that is toxic to the body.

Magnesium

Magnesium is essential in 350 enzyme reactions and indirectly required for thousands of others. Without adequate magnesium, your mental and physical health suffers greatly. Magnesium and Vitamin B6 must be present or the body cannot assimilate and properly use amino acids. Despite its importance, different sourc-

Symptoms of Magnesium Deficiency

- Anxiety
- Panic attacks
- Mitral valve prolapse
- Hypertension
- Chronic pain
- Back and neck pain
- Muscle spasms
- Migraines
- Fibromyalgia
- Spastic symptoms
- Chronic bronchitis, emphysema
- Vertigo (dizziness)
- Confusion
- Depression
- Psychosis
- Noise sensitivity
- Ringing in the ears
- Irritable bowel syndrome
- Cardiovascular disease
- Cardiac arrhythmias
- Atherosclerosis/Intermittent claudication
- Raynaud's disease (cold hands and feet)
- TIA's (Transient ischemic attacks-strokes)
- Constipation
- Fatigue
- Diabetes
- Hypoglycemia
- Asthma
- Seizures
- Kidney stones
- Osteoporosis

es report eighty to ninety percent of the population is magnesium deficient. In the alcoholic population the statistics are closer to one hundred percent. Magnesium depletion can cause the symptoms of horror or DTs (delirium tremors).

Magnesium is the number one mineral needed to combat stress. Magnesium plays an important role in controlling anxiety. When you are under stress, whether mental or physical, your body requires even higher levels of magnesium. The release of stress hormones causes an incredible increase in magnesium dependent reactions. This quickly depletes magnesium stores creating further magnesium deficiencies.

The body needs magnesium for muscle relaxation. Your body has 657 muscles that need magnesium every second of every day. The heart, your body's most important muscle, contracts and relaxes thousands of times a day. Without sufficient magnesium your heart can go into spasm causing death. Studies show people with low magnesium levels who have a heart attack are more apt to die than those whose magnesium level is adequate. Low magnesium levels interfere with your ability to sleep and causes high blood pressure, irregular heartbeats, spasms, and makes you irritable.

Supplementing with magnesium is safe and essential. *If you have impaired kidney function, you should not supplement with magnesium without consulting your physician first.* Magnesium can cause loose stools or diarrhea in some people. If this happens to you, try taking smaller doses or spread your doses out over three or four times a day.

At the Pain & Stress Center, we use magnesium chloride products called called Mag Link or Mag Chlor. The magnesium chloride form is more bioavailable as it works at the cellular level, and has better absorption and tolerance than other forms of magnesium.

Calcium

Alcoholism is a mineral wasting disease. Twenty minutes after drinking one ounce of alcohol, urinary calcium output increases by 100 percent, while magnesium increases to 167 percent. This causes severe deficiencies of these minerals. You may not experience deficiency symptoms until you stop drinking.

Low calcium levels cause painful leg cramps, insomnia, nervousness, and emotional instability. Low calcium levels are also related to high cholesterol levels and osteoporosis. While calcium has received a lot of press about its importance in bone health; magnesium is just as necessary for the prevention of osteoporosis.

Zinc

Zinc is required for protein synthesis and promotes a healthy immune system. It protects the liver from chemical damage and is vital for bone formation. Zinc deficiencies have been associated with sexual dysfunction and prostate gland enlargement and prostate cancer.

Use Cal Mag Zinc or Zinc Picolinate in capsule form for better absorption.

Super Pancreatin 650

A major effect of chronic alcohol consumption is damage to the entire digestive tract. The pancreas produces pancreatin, an enzyme, necessary for digestion that is greatly affected. Damage to the pancreas leads to malabsorption. When you stop drinking, this damage is not immediately reversed. You must supply pancreatic enzymes to reduce stress on the pancreas as well as improve your ability to absorb nutrients. Pancreatic enzymes are necessary for the healing process to begin.

Decaf Green Tea Extract

In the past few years a great deal of research shows that green tea has many health benefits. Green tea extract is a convenient way to receive all the health benefits of this potent antioxidant. We prefer the decaffeinated form with 95 percent EGCG (Epigallocatechin Gallate) polyphenols. Decaf green tea extract supports immune function and reduces inflammation. Green tea extract contains flavonoids that strengthen capillaries improving blood flow to the brain.

L-Theanine

L-theanine (L-T®) is a free form amino acid found in green tea leaves. Although theaninine is a new amino acid, it is an important player in balancing brain chemistry. Theanine appears to have a role in the formation of the major inhibitory neurotransmitter GABA (Gamma Amino Butyric Acid). With its support of GABA production theanine helps to calm anxiety and panic.

A study published in the *Journal of Food Science & Technology* in 1999 confirms theanine has a significant effect on the release of the neurotransmitters, dopamine and serotonin. These two neurotransmitters have a positive effect on mood.

L-T produces a tranquilizing effect in the brain without drowsiness or dull feelings. In fact, research has shown that theanine increases alpha waves in the brain. Of the four different types of brain waves, alpha waves denote a relaxed state of mental alertness like deep meditation.

For immediate relief from that *stressed out* feeling, open two L-Theanine capsules into small amount of water. Add a dropperful of Mag Chlor 85, and then four or five ounces of juice. This bedtime cocktail has profound effects inducing a relaxed, alert state in minutes. Although theanine does not cause sleepiness, using this combination 30 minutes before bedtime relaxes the mind and body that allows you to gently drift off to sleep.

Alpha-Lipoic Acid

Alpha-Lipoic Acid (ALA) is a super antioxidant. ALA has the power to regenerate other antioxidants like Vitamin C and E. ALA is water and fat soluble allowing it to reach virtually every tissue of the body. When the body has high levels of ALA and N-Acetyl Cysteine (NAC) as well as Vitamin C, it can make more glutathione, the body's endogenous antioxidant.

Alpha-Lipoic acid readily crosses the blood-brain barrier. Researchers hope ALA will help prevent diseases, like Alzheimer's and Parkinson's. Prevention of disease and slowing of the aging process is the real role of antioxidants.

Taurine

Taurine is classified as a conditionally essential amino acid. In adults, taurine is synthesized from cysteine and methionine, provided B-6 and zinc are present. Taurine is found throughout the body, in the heart muscle, olfactory bulb, central nervous system, and brain—specifically the hippocampus and pineal gland. Heart palpitations are common in people with low taurine levels.

Taurine is a key component of bile that is needed for the digestion of fats, the absorption of fat-soluble vitamins, and the control of serum cholesterol levels. Taurine is very helpful in the alcoholic. Certain metabolic disorders cause excessive losses of taurine through the urine. Cardiac arrhythmias, disorders of platelet formation, intestinal problems, an overgrowth of candida, stress, zinc deficiencies, and excessive consumption of alcohol cause high urinary loss of taurine. Excessive alcohol consumption causes the body to lose its ability to utilize taurine properly. Taurine supplementation reduces the symptoms of alcohol withdrawal by reducing muscle pain, tremor, and shaking. Taurine calms the mind.

For specific amino acids or nutrients, go to http://www.painstresscenter.com or call 1-800-669-2256.

11
Withdrawal Support
It's All About Nutrition

Alcoholism takes a horrible toll on physical health. Dr. Joseph Beasley compares the health status of an alcoholic to someone who has been in a train wreck. An average of twenty years of life is lost by practicing alcoholics according to a 1989 report in *Alcohol World* from National Institute on Alcohol Abuse and Alcoholism. Alcoholics generally die before age sixty-five from cirrhosis of the liver, heart disease, or several types of cancer commonly associated with alcoholism. Among young alcoholics, the death rates from suicide and accidents are ten times higher than normal.

While the statistics about alcoholic mortality are probably to be expected, studies have shown the death rate among recovered alcoholics is almost as high as it is among those who continue to drink. Why? Although no studies have been done, I would guess it is due to the failure of traditional treatment programs to address the issues of nutrition. Recovering alcoholics stop the abuse of alcohol, but fail to repair and rebuild damaged cells. The withdrawal supplements recommended in this book will decrease craving and begin the repair process.

In the previous chapter, we talked about all the nutrients that are helpful in the recovery of alcoholism. Over the past twenty years, I have developed many different formulas that combine specific amino acids and nutrients. They are in the proper balance and amounts for predictable results and ease of use. Use these supplements for the withdrawal program. If you are taking certain medications like SSRI's (selective serotonin reuptake inhibitors), tricyclics, or MAOI antidepressants, some of the supplements are not appropriate for you to take. If you are on medications that prevent you from using some of these amino acids, consider coming off them at some time. These drugs, just like alcohol, affect neurotransmitters levels. They do not provide the raw materials the brain needs to make more neurotransmitters and ultimately, cause further deficiencies. My book, *Break Your Prescribed Addiction*, is a helpful resource if you need to come off antidepressant or anti-anxiety medications.

As you look at all the supplements needed you might think this program is too costly. Well, think again. If you are honest about what you have spent on alcohol for just the past year, not to mention missed days of work, and the damage to your health, this program is cheap. High levels of nutrients are not required forever. As your total nutritional profile and health improves, you can reduce and tailor the supplements to your specific needs. Most recovered alcoholics find it beneficial to continue using some supplements to stay healthy and nourish the brain.

NOTE: The nutrient section is broken into 3 parts, Withdrawal Period to 3 months Post Sobriety, Maintenance Program, and Optional Nutrients. See next page for Withdrawal Program.

Optional Supplements

Glutamine – Any time you develop an alcohol craving, open a glutamine capsule and pour directly into the mouth.

Candex – If candida overgrowth is a problem, take 2 capsules twice daily as directed on the bottle.

DHEA – DHEA, the mother hormone, is the precursor of all steroid hormones, including estrogen, testosterone and cortisone. Produced by the adrenal glands it is the most abundant hormone in the body. Age, stress, pain and certain diseases can decrease DHEA levels dramatically. Studies, in which participants supplemented with DHEA reported an improved ability to cope with stress, had greater mobility, improved quality of sleep, and less joint pain. Additionally, they reported a seventy-five (75) percent increase in their overall well-being. Many alcoholics have low DHEA levels. DHEA levels can easily be tested to determine needs.

Nutrient and Amino Acid Program for Withdrawal Period and 3 Months Post Sobriety

Brain Link Complex *OR*	2 scoops, twice daily, morning, afternoon.
S.B.N.C	2 capsules, twice daily.
Mood Sync *OR* Anxiety Control *(WARNING: If you are taking an S.S.R.I., tricyclic, or MAO antidepressant, do not use Mood Sync. Instead, use Anxiety Control, 2 capsules, three times daily + L–T, 1 to 2 capsules, three times per day.)*	2 capsules, three times daily.
Glutamine (Caps or Powder)	Use 2 (500 mg) glutamine capsules, three times daily *OR* 1000 mg of glutamine powder, three to four times daily.
Mag Link *OR* Mag Chlor 85 *[WARNING: If loose stools or diarrhea occurs, decrease dose by 1 capsule (or number of drops) or increase time between doses.]*	2 capsules, three times daily *OR* 15 to 25 drops of Mag Chlor, three times daily.
T–L Vite (Not needed, if using Brain Link)	1 capsule with noon meal.
Rodex B6 Forte	1 capsule in morning.
ProDHA *OR* Pure Fish Oil Caps *WARNING: Do not use if you take anticoagnulants (blood thinners).*	2 capsules, twice daily.
DLPA *WARNING: Do not use if you have PKU (Phenylketonuria), taking a MAO or Tricyclic antidepressant, or have a history or cancer or melanoma.)*	1 capsule (750 mg), three times daily, divided.
Decaf Green Tea Extract	2 capsules, twice daily.
Ester C	2 (500 mg), twice daily.
Alpha Lipoic Acid	1 (300 mg) in afternoon.
Sleep Link *OR* 5-HTP *(WARNING: If you are taking an S.S.R.I., tricyclic, or MAO antidepressant, do not use Sleep Link or 5-HTP. Instead, use Anxiety Control, 2 capsules, L–T, 1 to 2 capsules, or a 3 mg Melatonin capsule.)*	2 capsules, 30 minutes before bed. If needed, add 1 melatonin 3 mg capsule or Mellow Mind (ashwagandha).

Taurine – Taurine greatly reduces the symptoms of alcohol withdrawal. Take 1 (1,000mg) capsule three times daily while detoxing, thereafter, one capsule daily.

Chromium Picolinate – Chromium is an essential mineral. It is involved in the metabolism of glucose, helping the body to maintain stable blood sugar. It is needed for the production of energy and is vital in the synthesis of cholesterol, fats, and proteins. If you are hypoglycemic, chromium is an important mineral for you. Chromium deficiency can lead to anxiety, fatigue, glucose intolerance, inadequate metabolism of amino acids and an increased risk of arteriosclerosis.

Sulfonil – Sulfonil contains patented thioglycerols that bind to the nicotine cell receptor sites preventing nicotine from attaching, thereby minimizing the desire to smoke. Unlike nicotine patches or gum that can increase blood pressure and pose the risk of addiction, Sulfonil has no side effects. This is is a safe, proven tool to help you stop smoking. *But don't try to conquer all your addictions at once, work on the alcohol first, then your sugar or smoking habit.*

Endorphins and enkephalins are two groups of structurally similar inhibitory neurotransmitters. Both effect pain & behavior. Alcohol mimics the effects of endorphins and enkephalins.

Alcohol Maintenance Program Nutrients

Brain Link Complex **OR**	2 scoops, in the morning
T–L Vite	1 capsule with noon meal
S.B.N.C	2 capsules, twice daily
Mood Sync **OR** Anxiety Control *(WARNING: If you are taking an S.S.R.I., tricyclic, or MAO antidepressant, do not use Mood Sync. Instead, use Anxiety Control, 2 capsules, three times daily + L–T, 1 to 2 capsules, three times per day.)*	2 capsules, three times daily
Glutamine (Caps or Powder)	Use 2 (500 mg) glutamine capsules, three times daily **OR** 1000 mg of glutamine powder, three to four times daily
Mag Link **OR** Mag Chlor 85 [*WARNING:* If loose stools or diarrhea occurs, decrease dose by 1 capsule (or number of drops) or increase time between doses.]	2 capsules, three times daily **OR** 15 to 25 drops of Mag Chlor, three times daily.
ProDHA **OR** Pure Fish Oil Caps *WARNING: Do not use if you take anticoagnulants (blood thinners).*	2 capsules, daily
DLPA (*WARNING: Do not use if you have PKU (Phenylketonuria), taking a MAO or Tricyclic antidepressant, or have a history or cancer or melanoma.*)	1 capsule (750 mg), twice daily, divided.
Decaf Green Tea Extract	2 capsules, twice daily.
Ester C	2 (500 mg), twice daily.
Alpha Lipoic Acid	1 (300 mg) in afternoon.
Sleep Link **OR** 5-HTP *(WARNING: If you are taking an S.S.R.I., tricyclic, or MAO antidepressant, do not use Sleep Link or 5-HTP. Instead, use Anxiety Control, 2 capsules, L–T, 1 to 2 capsules, or a 3 mg Melatonin capsule.)*	2 capsules, 30 minutes before bed.

12
Beyond Supplements

We have talked a lot about nutritional supplements. You might have the mistaken idea that all you need to do is take the recommended supplements and all will be well. While the supplements are essential to recovery several other components are necessary for success. You must eat a healthy diet and remove sugar, caffeine, and nicotine from your life; these are the final keys to success. Before you slam this book shut, throw it against the wall and give up, please read on. You don't have to quit drinking, smoking, and coffee all at the same time. Several different treatment centers demonstated that eliminating these stimulants along with alcohol makes a huge difference in your success. Not only will you finally be free of the need for alcohol, you can experience joy in life with some emotional stability.

Your brain has the ability to make the most wonderful *feel good* chemicals. You must provide it with the raw materials with a healthy diet and proper supplements so you can make the neurotransmitters you need. If you continue to flood the brain with false mood (addictive) chemicals such as sugar, caffeine, and nicotine, these chemicals trick your brain into thinking it has enough, and decreases production of the good mood chemicals and neurotransmitters. If you cannot control your sugar, caffeine, or nicotine intake all at once, focus on your alcohol now. Later, take on each addiction and conquer it.

Diet

Most alcoholics eat a horrible diet, skipping meals, living on sugar and junk food. Eating like this perpetuates the craving for alcohol. In order to stay sober, it is very important to eat a healthy diet that contains quality protein, lots of fresh vegetables, healthy carbohydrates, fresh fruits, and good fats. You need to eat three meals a day with two or three healthy snacks in between to keep your brain chemistry on track. This is not optional. Skipping meals or eating a diet high in sugar and processed foods keeps you on a hypoglycemic roller coaster that makes it difficult to stay sober.

Sugar

Sugar, caffeine, and nicotine interact negatively with our own brain chemistry. While it is common knowledge that caffeine and nicotine are addictive, sugar usually comes as a complete surprise to most people. Biochemically, sugar and alcohol are almost identical. Individuals who eat large amounts of sugar react emotionally in the same ways as alcoholics tending to be moody and unstable. The hypoglycemia cycle from high sugar foods causes blood sugars to drop increasing the need for more sugar. This quickly short-circuits your sobriety.

As you start on the supplements, *you must take enough glutamine to diminish your sugar cravings.* Limit your intake of sugar and learn what foods are laden with sugar. Sugar is disguised by many different names. You can easily be deceived by the food industry attempt to hide sugar. You need to become a label reader and stay away from foods that list sugar (especially, sucrose, corn syrup, dextrose, glucose) in the first four ingredients.

While we are on the subject of sugar, you need to know we do not recommend the use of aspartame (NutraSweet) as a substitute for sugar. Aspartame contains aspartic acid and phenylalanine. Aspartic acid is a major excitatory neurotransmitter and when taken along with phenylalanine, competes with tryptophan for absorption, effectively reducing serotonin levels. Common complaints from the use of NutraSweet are headache, bloating, depression, irritability, confusion, anxiety, insomnia, and phobias.

Caffeine

People who drink a lot of caffeine are usually low in the group of neurotransmitters called the catecholamines. When you have an abundance of catecholamines, you feel energized, upbeat, and alert. When you don't have enough of them, you go searching for something like caffeine to give you a boost. Caffeine increases your mood, but only for a short time. Caffeine triggers a stress reaction in the body that leads to high cortisol levels and eventually, adrenal exhaustion. This leaves you tired and worn out, and you go looking for more caffeine. When you flood your brain with artificial stimulants, the brain does not make the neurotransmitters it needs.

If you are a coffee or caffeinated soda drinker, tyrosine, the amino acid, comes to the rescue. Phenylalanine and tyrosine are what the body uses to make the catecholamines. As their levels increase naturally, you won't need stimulants to keep you alert.

Nicotine

Nicotine is bad on several counts. Besides the obvious health risks, nicotine is a stimulant. Nicotine use short circuits the appetite causing you to skip meals and that leads to hypoglycemia and alcohol craving. The addiction to nicotine happens in the brain—just as with sugar and caffeine. Nicotine replaces your neurotransmitters. You cannot completely balance brain chemistry if you are using substances that react at neurotransmitter receptor sites.

Tobacco is cured with sugar. Smoking, chewing, or dipping tobacco increases blood sugar levels that end with a hypoglycemic episode. It is difficult for you to gain control of your blood sugar, if you are using tobacco in any form. Use a product called Sulfonil to stop the craving for nicotine along with some Vitamin C. Sulfonil is a patented formula that actually binds to the nicotine receptor sites; thereby, reducing the craving for nicotine. Vitamin C helps your body to detoxify nicotine moving it out of your system sooner.

The Cortisol Connection

Stress and the overproduction of cortisol is another compelling reason to stop sugar, caffeine and nicotine. The adrenal glands are two small triangular shaped organs that rest on top of the kidneys. The adrenals produce many different hormones, but the two most familiar, are adrenaline and cortisol. These are commonly called the *fight or flight* hormones.

In an emergency situation, adrenaline releases to prepare you for action, followed by cortisol that subdues the effects of adrenaline, and infuses you with strength and stamina. In an emergency situation these two hormones are life saving. But when stress is on-going, these hormones keep you in an over-excited emotional state that leads to other significant health problems. Initially, high cortisol levels cause weight gain, reduction in energy levels, a decrease in sex drive, and loss of memory. Over time these potentially evolve into obesity, diabetes, impotence, dementia, heart disease, and cancer.

Besides the health risks, high cortisol levels have a direct effect on mood, increase irritability, decrease concentration and increase depression and anxiety. These mental states promote alcohol craving. Besides the normal stress of being alive, guess what chronically increases cortisol levels? Diets high in refined sugar and carbohydrates, nicotine, and caffeine! Understanding the negative effects that these stimulants have on the brain helps you to stay away from them so you can maintain your sobriety more easily.

13
Getting Started

The first step to recovery is to begin on the supplements recommended in the last chapter. Many recovering alcoholics will say they can't afford all those supplements and which *one* supplement can they take to make it all go away. It just doesn't work that way—there is no one single, magical pill that can repair your damaged biochemistry. If you take all the supplements recommended as well as following a healthy diet, you will quickly see results. You will notice a decrease of cravings along with a gradual return of your overall health.

If you are still drinking, begin taking your supplements for a week before you stop drinking. You will notice a decrease in your desire to drink once you begin on the program. Some people find it helpful to stop drinking on Friday night. This gives you the weekend to go through any withdrawal symptoms you might experience. Other people have found it is easier to stop during the week. Whatever you decide, using the supplement program greatly reduces, if not completely resolves, most withdrawal symptoms.

If you stop drinking over a weekend, make sure you have someone with you for support. By yourself, it is too easy to decide one more drink won't hurt, or perhaps next weekend would be a better time to quit. Your support person helps to distract you so you don't just sit around all weekend and obsess about alcohol. They can also be there in case of any medical emergency.

Depending on the severity of your drinking problem, you may need to go to an inpatient treatment program to detox. Unfortunately, most inpatient programs are still in the dark ages about the importance of nutritional support. If you are able to plan your entrance, we still recommend starting on the supplements for five days prior to going to detox. Take your supplements with you if they will allow it. If not, start back on the supplements as soon as you return home.

Beyond Supplements
Strategies For Maintaining Sobriety

With the nutritional support program we have outlined, you are on your way to a life free of the physical craving for alcohol. As much as we have talked about the biochemistry of alcohol, psychological triggers will bring your new found sobriety crashing down if you are not prepared with a total life plan. The following are some important suggestions for avoiding common pit falls.

Alcoholics Anonymous

Having a support system that encourages your new sobriety is vital to recovery. Family and friends can be helpful. However the encouragement of someone who has walked in your shoes is invaluable. Alcoholics Anonymous (AA) is an organization of men and women of all ages and backgrounds who are actively committed to their sobriety as well as yours.

AA is the original 12-step program. The 12-step formula developed by Alcoholics Anonymous has been very successful in helping people to gain control of their lives. Working the steps, as they refer to the active participation in the program, can be the foundation for emotional and spiritual healing.

Local AA chapters exist in every city and town. Look in your phone book to find a meeting near you.

Friends

Everyone needs friends. If you are newly sober and the only friends you have are your old drinking buddies, you are headed for trouble. Now is a good time to make new, non-drinking friends. There are many good places to meet new people. Work, church, AA meetings, and neighbors are a good starting place.

Exercise

Exercise does wonders for the brain and body. Exercise increases oxygen levels to the brain, strengthens the heart, reduces blood sugar, raises self-esteem and elevates mood. No other single investment of time has such great returns. Find a physical activity that you enjoy, and do it at least four or more times a week. The choices for exercise are endless; you can walk, ride a bicycle, swim, garden, play tennis, dance, or whatever you like doing. Regular exercise greatly enhances your health and enjoyment of life.

Body & Brain Profile Tests
To Balance the Brain & Body Chemistry

1. Amino Acid Testing

The body constantly conducts many complicated series of chemical reactions in precisely controlled ways to keep us healthy. Over 5,000 reactions occur every second in each individual cell. The absence of even one needed nutrient can have profound effects on your overall health. You can correct the cause of some disease processes in a nontoxic way by supplying natural substances in optimal quantities to reestablish a normal balance.

Amino acid metabolism disorders are becoming recognized as a major factor in many disease processes. Amino acid analysis is an analytical technique on the leading edge of nutritional biochemical medicine. It gives a new approach toward illness, and assists patients who have not responded to treatment as expected, or who present complex cases with diverse symptoms.

Amino acid analysis of urine or blood plasma goes a long way toward assessing vitamin and mineral status. Amino acid analysis measures the levels of amino acids in the body that affect many important processes. Additionally, it provides insights into the patient's functional needs for a wide variety of vitamins and minerals. Many of the enzymes that catalyze the interconversion of amino acids require vitamin and mineral cofactors to function optimally.

Amino acid analysis has proven helpful in treating:

- Alcoholism
- ADD/Hyperactivity
- Arthritis
- Behavior disorders
- Chronic fatigue
- Candida infections
- Cancer
- Cardiovascular disease
- Depression
- Diabetes
- Eating disorders
- Food and chemical intolerances.
- Headaches
- Hypoglycemia
- Immune system
- Learning disorders
- Seizures

2. Food Allergy Profile

Food allergies are a common problem for people who have addiction tendencies or dependence. The test reports over 100 foods, sensitivity rating and gives you a complete diet to follow.

3. Essential Fatty Acid Profile

EFAs are vital to brain function, correcting mood disorders, depression and gastrointestinal problems. The test provides an analysis of the EFAs currently present and a guide to the amounts needed.

4. Comprehensive Vitamin Profile

This profile provides a complete analysis of 17 vitamins and specific amounts needed by your brain and body. This test helps establish your deficiency problems.

5. DHEA Sulfate Level

DHEA is the Mother Hormone because it is the precursor of all steroid hormones including estrogen, testosterone, and cortisol. Aging, stress, pain, depression, anxiety and certain diseases cause your DHEA level to drop drastically.

The drop in DHEA compounds your body's ability to respond to stresses, diseases, and makes you age more rapidly. If you are over 40, you should have your DHEA level checked.

Consider adding DHEA to your supplement program first thing in the morning if you are over 40. DHEA is available in capsule form or in a transdermal cream.

> For information on testing, call
> Pain & Stress Managment Clinic at
> 1-800-669-2256, Monday through Friday,
> 8:30 A.M. to 5 P.M., Central Time.

Bibliography

Agharanya J. C., Alonso R and Wurtman R.J. "Tyrosine loading enhances catecholamines excretion by rats." *Journal of Neural Transmission*, Vol. 49, 1980, pp. 41–43.

Appleton, Nancy. *Lick The Sugar Habit*. Garden City Park, NY: Avery Publishing Group, 1996.

Balch, James F. and Phyllis A. Balch, *Prescription for Nutritional Healing*, Garden City Park, NY: Avery Publishing, 1997.

Beasley, Joseph D. *How To Defeat Alcoholism*. New York, NY: Times Books, 1989.

Blum, Kenneth and Michael C Trachtenberg. *Some Things You Should Know About Alcoholism*. Houston TX: Matrix Technologies, Inc. 1988.

Blum, Kenneth and Michael C. Trachtenberg. "Neuro-chemistry and Alcohol Craving." *California Society for the Treatment of Alcoholism and Other Drug Dependencies News*. September, 1986, pp. 1–7.

Braverman, Eric R, and Carl C Pfeiffer. *The Healing Nutrients Within*. New Canaan, CT: Keats Publishing, 1987.

Cadoret, R.J. "Development of Alcoholism in Adoptees Raised Apart from Alcoholic Biological Relatives."*Archives of General Psychiatry*, Vol. 37, 1980, pp. 561–563.

Crespi F, Ratti E, and Trist D.G. "Melatonin, a hormone monitorable in vivo by voltammetry." *Analyst* 1994; Vol. 119, No. 10, pp. 2193–97.

Donsbach, Kurt W, Sandy Shaw, and Durk Pearson. *What You Always Wanted to Know About Alcohol*. The International Institute of Natural Health Sciences, Inc. 1980.

Ellis, John, M. and Jean Pamplin. *Vitamin B6 Therapy*. Garden City Park, NY: Avery Publishing Group, 1999.

Gavrielli, W.F., et al. "Electroencephalograms in Children of Alcoholic Fathers." *Psychophysiology*, Vol. 19, No. 4 (1982), pp. 404–407.

Goodwin, D.W. "Alcoholism and Heredity," *Archives of General Psychiatry* Vol. 36, 1979, pp. 57–61.

Guenther, R.M. "The Role of Nutritional Therapy in Alcoholism Treatment." *International Journal of Biosocial Research*, Vol. 4, No. 1, 1983, pp. 5–18.

Haiken, Melanie "A Better Way to Treat Alcoholism." *Alternative Medicine Magazine*. February 2004, pp. 77–80, 118–123.

Jensen, Bernard. *Dr. Jensen's Guide To Body Chemistry & Nutrition*. Lincolnwood, IL: Keats Publishing, 2000.

Kotulak, Ronald. *Inside the Brain*. Kansas City, MO: Andrew McMeel, 1996.

Larson, Joan Mathews. S*even Weeks to Sobriety*. New York, NY: Random House Publishing, 1997.

Lehnert H, Reinstein D.K., Strowbridge BW, and Wurtman R.J. "Neurochemical and behavioral consequences of acute, uncontrollable stress: Effects of dietary tyrosine." *Brain Research* 1984,Vol. 303, pp. 215–23.

Lieber C.S. "Biochemical and molecular basis of alcohol-induced injury to liver and other tissues."*New England Journal of Medicine* Vol. 391 No.25, pp. 639–1650, 1988.

Meletis, Chris D. and Elizabeth Wagner. "Alternative Treatment for Alcoholism." *Natural Pharmacy*, December 2003, pp. 18–19.

Miller, Norman S., et al. (Ed.) Manual of Therapeutics for Addictions. New York: John Wiley & Sons, 1997, pp. 3–40.

Murray, Michael. *5-HTP The Natural Way to Overcome Depression, Obesity, and Insomnia.* New York, NY: Bantam Books, 1998.

Nestler, Eric J. and Robert Malenka. "The Addicted Brain." *Scientific American,* March 2004, pp. 76–85.

Pell, S. and C.D. Alonzo. "A Five Year Mortality Study of Alcoholics," *Journal of Occupational Medicine*, Feb. 1973, pp. 120–125.

Pheiffer, Carl C. *Nutrition and Mental Illness.* Rochester, VT: Healing Arts Press, 1975.

Phelps, Janice Keller. *The Hidden Addiction and How to Get Free.* New York, NY: Marlowe & Co. 1999.

Rogers, Sherry, A. *No More Heartburn Stop the Pain In 30 Days-Naturally!* New York, NY: Kensington Publishing Corp., 2000.

"Roots of Addiction." *Newsweek.* February 20, 1989, pp. 52–58.

Ross, Julia. *The Diet Cure.* New York, NY: The Penguin Group, 1999.

Ross, Julia. *The Mood Cure.* New York, NY: Penguin Putnam Inc., 2002.

Rudin, D.O., Felix, C. *The Omega-3 Phenomenon.* New York, NY: Rawson Associates, 1987.

Sahley, Billie Jay and Katherine Birkner. *Breaking Your Precribed Addiction.* San Antonio, TX: Pain & Stress Publications, 1998.

Sahley, Billie Jay and Katherine Birkner. *Break Your Precribed Addiction.* San Antonio, TX: Pain & Stress Publications, 2004.

Sahley, Billie Jay and Katherine Birkner. *Heal With Amino Acids and Nutrients.* San Antonio, TX: Pain & Stress Publications, 2001.

Smith, Russell. "A Five-Year Trial of Massive Nicotinic Acid Therapy of Alcoholics in Michigan," *Journal of Orthomolecular Psychiatry* 3(1974):327–31.

Talbott, Shawn. *The Cortisol Connection.* Alameda CA: Hunter House Publishers, 2002.

Tumiel, Cindy. "Gene That May Raise Risk of Alcoholism is Identified." *San Antonio Express-News*, January 15, 2004, p. 3 A.

Wolff, P.H. "Ethnic Differences in Alcohol Sensitivity." *Science* Vol. 175, 1972 pp. 449–450.

Index

Symbols

5-HTP (5-hydroxy-tryptophan) 45–46

A

AA 52
acetaldehyde 21, 41
ADD 18, 47, 53–55
addiction, heroin 32
adrenaline 25, 46
adrenal gland 50. 61
aggression 27–28
aggressive behavior 45
ALA 52
Alcoholics Anonymous (AA) 70
alcohol craving 41–42, 44, 47–52, 61, 67
alcohol dehydrogenase 20
Alpha-linolenic acid (ALA) 52–53
alpha waves 58
Alzheimer's disease 54
amino acids 23, 33, 40, 44–53, 54, 58, 60, 63, 72
amino acid analysis 72
amino acid testing 72
amphetamines 48
anti-anxiety 61
anti-inflammatory 53
anti-stress 50
antibiotics 41
antidepressant 43, 60–64
antioxidant 49, 50, 57
anxiety 9, 20, 26–27, 36, 42, 44, 47, 54–58
Anxiety Control 28

Arachidonic acid (AA) 52–53
arteriosclerosis 63
ashwaganda 62
asthma 55
Ativan 24, 47
Attention Deficit Disorder (A.D.D.) 9, 18, 42
auto-brewery syndrome 41

B

BCAA (Branch Chain Amino Acids) 49
Beasley, Joseph 18, 24, 35, 44
benzodiazepines 47
biochemistry 9, 69
bipolar disorder 26, 53
blood-brain barrier 24, 45
blood sugar 38–40, 50, 63
brain chemistry 20, 44, 67
brain function 51, 58
branched-chain amino acids (BCAA) 49
Break Your Prescribed Addiction 61
breath-a-lyzer 41
B Vitamins 51–52

C

caffeine 65, 67
calcium 56–58
calm 26, 44, 46–47
cancer 47, 48, 60, 62, 64
Candex 41
candida 41, 59, 61
canola oil 52
cardiac arrhythmias 55, 59
cardiovascular disease 55
catecholamines 32, 46–47, 67
cerebral cortex 54
chemical messengers 24
cholesterol 56, 63
chromium 40, 63
chronic pain 45, 55
cirrhosis 47, 49, 60
cocaine 24, 42
coffee 46
concentration 46–47
confusion 55
cortisol 67
cortisone 61

D

deficiencies 51–58
dementias 54
depression 9, 27, 36, 42, 44–48, 53–56
DHA (docosahexaenoic acid) 52–55
DHEA 61, 73
diabetes 55
digestive tract 48, 57
DLPA 44, 48–49
Docosahexaenoic acid (DHA) 52, 55
dopamine 44, 46, 54, 58
drug abuse 12
DTs (delirium tremors) 54

E

EFAs 73
EGCG (Epigallocatechin Gallate) 57
Eicosapentaenoic acid (EPA) 52
emotional instability 56
EMS (eosinophilia-myalgia syndrome) 45

endorphins 24, 32, 44, 47, 51
enkephalins 24
enzymes 50, 54, 57
eosinophilia-myalgia syndrome (EMS) 45
EPA (eicosapentaenoic acid) 52
epinephrine 43
Essential Fatty Acid 73
essential fatty acids (EFAs) 52–53
Ester C 51
estrogen 61
euphoria 27, 44, 48
excitatory messages 47

F

fats 40, 52–54, 63
feel good chemicals 44, 46, 65
fibromyalgia 55
fish oil supplements 53
flavonoids 57
folic acid 50
food allergy 73

G

GABA (Gamma Amino Butyric Acid) 20, 22, 26–27, 44–47, 58
Gamma-linolenic acid (GLA) 52
genetic 10, 18, 19–21, 24, 48
GLA 52
glucose 38, 50, 63
glutamine 40, 48–49, 66
glutathione 49
glycine 40
Green Tea Extract 57
Griffonia seeds 45

H

hangover 20
HDL 11
heart 52, 56, 60
heart palpitations 59
heroin 24, 32
heroin addicts 50
high blood pressure 48, 56
hypertension 55
hypoglycemia 36, 39, 55, 66, 67
hypoglycemic 63

I

immune system 49, 52
impaired kidney function 56
inflammation 52–54, 52, 57
insomnia 45, 56
insulin 38–39
irregular heartbeats 56
irritability 45, 56
isoleucine 49

K

kidney stones 55
Klonopin 47
Koob, George Dr. 21

L

L-theanine (L-T) 58
LDL cholesterol 11
leg cramps 56
leucine 49
Lexapro 45
Le Doux, Joseph 23
Libby, Alfred 50
Librium 47
limbic system 21–22
Linoleic acid (LA) 52–53
liver 49, 51
liver enzyme 20

M

magnesium 35, 54–58
magnesium deficiencies 36, 54–55
Mag Link 56
MAO 46–47, 48, 60, 62–64
marijuana 42
master controller 46
medication, prescribed 42
melanoma 47, 48
melatonin 46
mental disorders 42
migraines 55–56
Mitral valve prolapse 55
muscle relaxation 56
muscle spasms 36, 55

N

National Institute of Health (NIH) 49
neurological 36
neurons 23
neurotransmitters 9–10, 18, 23–24, 26, 32, 42–54, 58, 60–63, 65, 67
neurotransmitter deficiency 45
niacin 35, 51
nicotine 24, 46, 63, 65, 67
NMDA receptor 26
norepinephrine 23, 46

O

omega-3 52–54
omega-6 52–54
orthomolecular 5, 43
osteoporosis 55, 57

P

pain 42
painkillers 24, 44
pancreas 36, 39, 49, 57
pancreatic enzymes 57–58
pancreatitis 36
panic attacks 26, 55
Pauling, Linus 43
Paxil 24, 45
PEA (phenylethylamine) 48
Pfeiffer, Carl, 43
phenylalanine 50, 66–67
PKU (Phenylketonuria) 48
pleasure center 21, 24–25
polyphenols 57
Post Synaptic Receptor 23
Prednisone 41
ProDHA 54
Prozac 24, 45
pseudo-brain chemicals 24
psychological 18, 33
psychosis 55

R

receptor 23–24
receptor sites 26
reuptake 24–25
reward system 21, 26
Rogers, Sherry M.D. 41
Ross, Julia M.A. 54
Rudin, Donald 53

S

schizophrenic 47
seizures 55
Selective Serotonin Reuptake Inhibitors (SSRIs) 46
serotonin 23, 27, 43, 44–46, 58
serotonin deficiency 45
sleep 32, 46
Smith, Russell, M.D. 51
smoking 63
SSRIs (Selective Serotonin Reuptake Inhibitor) 45
stimulants 46–47, 65, 67
Stone, Irwin W. 50
stop switch 26
stress 9, 24, 27, 46–48, 54, 61
sugar 35, 39, 41, 66
sugar cravings 66
suicide 60
Sulfonil 67
Super Balanced Neurotransmitter Complex (SBNC) 50
supplements 42, 60–61, 69
synapse 23–24, 53

T

taurine 59, 61
theanine 58
thiamine 51
tobacco 67
tranquilizers 47
trans fatty acids 52
tremors 36
tricyclic antidepressants 48
tryptophan 43, 44–46, 66
tyrosine 43–44, 50, 67

V

valine 49
Valium 47
Vitamin B1 (Thiamine) 51
Vitamin C 35, 50, 58

W

Wernicke-Korsakoff syndrome 51
Williams, Roger 48
withdrawal symptoms 32, 51, 69

X

Xanax 47

Y

yeast 41

Z

zinc 57, 59
Zoloft 45

Private Nutritional Consultation Service

With all the nutritional choices and dietary plans today, how do you pick the program that is right for you?

Do you want personalized, expert help in formulating a plan that is tailored to you and your particular needs?

Discuss your specific problems and needs with a Certified Nutritional Consultant one-on-one at *affordable* prices.

You can talk directly to a C.N.C. professional with experience and expertise in orthomolecular therapy and nutritional supplements.

- Sessions are personalize and confidential in the privacy of your home or office.
- Discuss your problems or specific goals and plans with a Certified Nutritional Counselor (C.N.C.).
- Expertise in orthomolecular therapy and nutritional supplements.
- Receive answers to your questions and concerns one-on-one.
- Receive support in moving your health toward your wellness goals.

Call 1-800-669-2256 To Schedule Your Personal Nutritional Consult!

Other Books From Pain & Stress Publications®

THE ANXIETY EPIDEMIC
How GABA and Other Amino Acids Are The Key To Controlling Anxiety and Panic Attacks
Billie Jay Sahley, Ph.D.

HEAL With AMINO ACIDS and Nutrients
Billie J. Sahley, Ph.D.
Kathy Birkner, C.R.N.A., Ph.D.

GABA The *Anxiety* Amino Acid
Revolutionary Discoveries of How GABA Affects Mind, Mood, Memory, and Behavior
Billie Jay Sahley, Ph.D.
Author of The Anxiety Epidemic

STOP A.D.D. NATURALLY

Cutting Edge Information On Amino Acids, Brain Function and A.D.D. Behavior
Billie J. Sahley, Ph.D., C.N.C.
Foreword By Doris Rapp, M.D.

BREAK Your PRESCRIBED ADDICTION
A Guide To Coming Off . . . Tranquilizers, Antidepressants (S.S.R.I.s, M.A.O.s) & More Using Amino Acids and Nutrients
Billie J. Sahley, Ph.D., C.N.C.
Katherine M. Birkner, C.R.N.A., Ph.D.

THEANINE the RELAXATION Amino Acid
Latest Research on Green Tea and Theanine—An Amazing New Amino Acid
Billie J. Sahley, Ph.D., C.N.C.
Author of The Anxiety Epidemic

Is Ritalin Necessary?
The Ritalin Report

Ritalin And Other Drugs Are NOT The Answer To A.D.D./A.D.H.D.
Amino Acids Offer Safe, Effective Natural Alternatives
Billie J. Sahley, Ph.D
Author of Stop A.D.D. Naturally

Post *Trauma* and Chronic *Emotional* Fatigue

Mind and Body Illnesses That Control Your Life!
Natural Answers For Healing and Recovery
Billie J. Sahley, Ph.D., C.N.C.

Malic Acid and Magnesium for Fibromyalgia
and Chronic Pain Syndrome
Understand Why You Hurt All Over And What You Can Take Naturally To Stop The Pain
Billie J. Sahley, Ph.D., C.N.C.

To Order Call 1-800-669-2256 or go to www.painstresscenter.com

About the Authors

Billie J. Sahley, Ph.D. is Executive Director of the Pain & Stress Center in San Antonio. She is a Board Certified Medical Psychotherapist/Behavior Therapist, and an Orthomolecular Therapist. She is a Diplomate in the American Academy of Pain Management. Dr. Sahley is a graduate of the University of Texas, Clayton University School of Behavioral Medicine, and U.C.L.A. School of Integral Medicine. Additionally, she has studied advanced nutritional biochemistry through Jeffrey Bland, Ph.D., Director of HealthComm. She is a member of the Huxley Foundation/Academy of Orthomolecular Medicine, Academy of Psychosomatic Medicine, North American Nutrition and Preventive Medicine Association. In addition, she holds memberships in the Sports Medicine Foundation, American Mental Health Counselors, and American Academy of Pain Management She also sits on the Scientific and Medical Advisory Board for Inter-Cal Corporation.

Dr. Sahley has written *The Anxiety Epidemic, Stop A.D.D. Naturally, Chronic Emotional Fatigue, Malic Acid and Magnesium for Fibromyalgia and Chronic Pain Syndrome, The Melatonin Report, GABA, the Anxiety Amino Acid, The Ritalin Report, Theanine, The Relaxation Amino Acid*. She has coauthored *Break Your Prescribed Addiction* and *Heal with Amino Acids*. In addition, she has recorded numerous audio cassette tapes on health related subjects.

Dr. Sahley holds three U.S. patents for Anxiety Control 24, SAF, and Calms Kids (SAF for Kids).

Katherine Birkner is a C.R.N.A., Pain Therapist at the Pain & Stress Center in San Antonio. She is a Registered Nurse, Certified Registered Nurse Anesthetist, Advanced Nurse Practitioner, Orthomolecular Therapist, and a Certified Nutritional Consultant. She is a Diplomate in American Academy of Pain Management. She attended Brackenridge Hospital School of Nursing, University of Texas at Austin, Southwest Missouri School of Anesthesia, Southwest Missouri State University and Clayton University. She holds degrees in nursing, nutrition, and behavior therapy. Dr. Birkner has done graduate studies through Center for Integral Medicine and U.C.L.A. Medical School. Additionally, she has studied advanced nutritional biochemistry through Jeffrey Bland, Ph.D., HealthComm. She is a member of The American Association of Nurse Anesthestists and American Academy of Pain Management. She is co-author of *Heal with Amino Acids and Break Your Prescribed Addiction*.

Jule Freeman is a Certified Nutritional Consultant, a Registered Massage Therapist, and Product Specialist at the Pain & Stress Center. She is dedicated to using natural alternatives to help people live drug-free!